The Builder's Companion
BOOK 1

ZERO TO BUILDING PERMIT
US/Canada Edition

Your Complete Guide to Home Building

PHILIP FITZPATRICK
A Builders Companion Series

Copyright © 2021 Balcombe Bay Publishing

All rights reserved. No part of this book may be reproduced, stored in a retrieval system or transmitted, in any form or by any means, without the prior written consent of the publishers, except in the case of brief quotations, embodied in reviews and articles. This publication contains the opinions and ideas of its author. It is intended to provide helpful and informative information on the subject matter covered. It is sold with the understanding that the author and publisher are not engaged in rendering professional services in this book. The author and publisher specifically disclaim any responsibility for the liability, loss or risk, personal or otherwise, which is incurred as a consequence, directly or indirectly, of the use and application of any of the contents of this book.

ISBN 978-0-6450959-0-6 (paperback)
ISBN 978-0-6450958-1-4 (e-book)

Published by Balcombe Bay Publishing. BBP

Also by Philip Fitzpatrick

The Builder's Companion
Book 2
Start Building to Certificate of Occupancy
US/Canada Edition
Manage and Build Your Home

The Builder's Companion
Book 1
Zero to Planning Permission
UK/Ireland Edition
Your Complete Guide to Home Building

The Builder's Companion
Book 2
Start Building to Completion Certificate
UK/Ireland Edition
Manage and Build Your Home

The Builder's Companion
Book 1
Zero to Planning Permit
Australia/New Zealand Edition
Your Complete Guide to Home Building

The Builder's Companion
Book 2
Start Building to Occupancy Permit
Australia/New Zealand Edition
Manage and Build Your Home

and published by Balcombe Bay Publishing BBP

Kickstart Your Project

Download Your FREE Bonus!

Scan the QR-code to access the

The Builder's Companion
Schedules and Charts Workbook

SCAN ME
https://abuilderscompanion.com/get-your-free-ebook

Download
The 1-Page Building Plan
Schedule of Works
The Players Chart
Project Milestones Chart
What Does it Do?
Build Cost Projection Budget
Good Practice Check Box
Defects (Punch) List
Finish Schedule

TABLE OF CONTENTS

Acknowledgments vii
Preface ix
Introduction xiii

Chapter 1   Jigsaw Puzzle 1
Chapter 2   Assessing Your Lot 23
Chapter 3   Define Your Requirements 53
Chapter 4   The Legal Bit 65
Chapter 5   The Players 79
Chapter 6   The Professionals – Consultants and Tradespeople 93
Chapter 7   Designer's Program & Permit Application 113
Chapter 8   Permit Granted 143
Chapter 9   Cost Control 151
Chapter 10   Money 175

Conclusion 193
General Glossary 195
Abbreviations 201
Services Abbreviations 207
Excavation Glossary 209
Professional Roles 211
Index 219
About the Author 221
Take-Aways 223
Do you feel 'Companionable'? 225

ACKNOWLEDGMENTS

Building is a team activity as is producing a book. Many people lend a hand and this is of greater benefit than they know. Their advice and the experiences they shared are greatly appreciated.

Books 1 & 2

Reviewers
Brendan Hoban	Founder, Hoban-Hynes, Melbourne Australia.
Alan O'Doherty	Lawyer & Realtor, Sotheby's International Realty, New York & Connecticut USA.
Paul Browne	Solicitor, London UK.
John Boecker	Architect, Author and Environmentalist, 7group / Boecker Consulting Services New Jersey USA.
Peter Hammond	Author, London UK.
Mark Fitzpatrick	Builder & Services Engineer, London UK.

Editor
Jennifer Lancaster   Power of Words, Brisbane Australia.

Architectural sketches
Pam Toan   Designer, Hoban-Hynes, Melbourne Australia.

PREFACE

Who is This Book For?

This book is written primarily with the enthusiastic home builder or their partner in mind. It has been my experience that in many relationships, one of the partners is the 'reader' and is ready with the facts, while the other is better at getting stuck in and doing things… never mind the instruction sheet!

Or perhaps you watch home building shows on television and dream of building a house yourself one day. If you simply want to know more about the process, I hope you will find some truth in my experience of construction and its world. I have been employed as a builder all my working life and been involved with thousands of properties and personally built seven family homes. I know that when people say that they cannot visualise what things will look like or that they do not have fixed views, with a little digging and illustration, with a visit to a showroom these fence sitters very quickly become passionate about how things should look. This passion is what we need to move the design and finish to the next higher level. The exciting design that works, the higher quality finish and the home that is truly 'yours' are reasons why we are bothering with this book.

Why Are You Intending to Owner-Build?

First, you should consider if owner-building is the right way forward for you.

Owner–building is much more than just construction. It's design, it's making modern technology fit into your home, it's accountancy, it's surveying and project management. Interestingly, the thing you need not concern yourself so much with at the early stages is how you actually build a home. After all, if you don't take care of these crucial elements and their budget, the actual build process just won't happen.

Who is Who in This Book?

As you will cover many different roles on the owner-build journey, I need to be clear who I am referring too.

The *Owner* is also the owner-builder, general contractor, project manager, bean-counter, materials scheduler, estimator, surveyor, cost engineer and often leading laborer and Jack-of-all-trades. For consistency, I will call you by the title 'owner-builder' (most of the time). In the end, the job's motto could be 'if in doubt, sort it out' and do not expect any thanks.

The *builder* can be the contractor, main contractor, general contractor or principal contractor.

A *trades contractor* can also be a contractor, a sub-contractor (subs or subbie) or a specialist contractor. While names and titles are all over the place, it is still best that a named person is in charge of a specific task.

Your lot is also known by many different names. It is referred to as a property or a block of land or simply 'a block' and when work commences, it becomes a construction site or building site or just 'a site'. The house built is known as a home or within the trades as a site… or job or job site!

Industry parlance doesn't end there. Local names apply to the term for planning permission; this is also known as *planning permit* or *development approval*. Again, you should go with local custom. They are all interchangeable and as long as you know what you mean and what is being said to you, you should be OK.

What This Book Is:

The information this book offers is not available in a single place on the internet. A jigsaw of information online is one thing, but this book brings experience only learned by doing it. This is experience I wish to share, so people can make better choices, build better buildings and have a less stressful journey through the owner-builder experience.

Advice is offered from the very start of the process, even before purchase of a specific lot.

After all, you need to know how to get your new house project started. It raises awareness of the importance of each and every phase of the work, from thinking through what it is you want, to achieving an actual building permit and getting the money in place. With this meld of information, you do not need to search all over the web or buy a library of books; it's all here.

It is an encouraging thought that owner-builder's are at the cutting edge of modern views on construction delivery. The American Institute of Architects (AIA) supports what it terms Integrated Project Delivery (IPD). This brings the builder into the design process from the earliest design stage, which improves efficiency and produces better buildings.

My passion for building is obvious. I have been employed and self-employed as a builder all my working life and even before. My father was a builder (as is my son) and I was taken to jobs to help and work, long before I left school. I saw enough of site life by the age of eleven to know I wanted to be a building surveyor. My grandson will be able to look back at photographs of visiting construction sites (safely) from before the age of 5 years as can his father!

I have not sugar-coated just how hard it can be to build your own home from scratch for the first time. It does get easier when you repeat the exercise but it's never *easy*. Think of this book as your 'builder's companion'.

Philip Fitzpatrick

SUMMARY

- Start your personalized 1-Page Owner-Builder Plan
- Think like a builder
- Be committed and inspire your team to become a 'crew'

INTRODUCTION

'A simple person can learn of things he has no fixed view on, an intelligent person cannot learn anything if he believes, without a shadow of a doubt, he already knows the answers'.

– Leo Tolstoy

This book is meant to be encouraging. It's my intention to encourage your excitement and self-belief so that you can join the millions of others from time immemorial who, owner-built their house.

I want you to save money by learning from my mistakes(!) while giving you a plan of how to get a better house.

The 'better' house can be larger, to suit your growing family, with higher quality features you may not be able to afford if purchasing from a house building company. Alternatively, the 'better' house may be a cheaper house of a comparable size and type you would normally purchase. Or again, you want something truly personal that reflects your lifestyle in the area you want to live.

How much you save is based on how you approach the build process. If saving money is your aim, this can be your target; if you want a better quality house, this can be your target. Consider a mix-and-match and get both; the choice is yours.

Saving time is an aspiration of many new owner-builders. Time savings can be achieved if you communicate clear instructions and follow a method of build management. But, time can only be based on a like-for-like basis. Purchasing a finished house is obviously the speediest way of moving in, so any reader of this book must be interested in something more than just time saving. This practical book will assist in you managing a quick and efficient build.

I am not concerned with what your actual approach to the build is. You are as 'right' if you carry out each and every task personally or if you employ a full-time site manager and builder and you attend at set times. Most people are somewhere in the middle. Regardless, my whole approach is to share a vision of how you proceed.

The 1-Page Owner-Builder Plan

One of the points made in this book is 'if you cannot write it down, you cannot do it'.

To assist, I have prepared a Build Plan.

This plan prompts you to make notes as you develop your project in an orderly way. This will give you a plan of attack while taking in the big picture. You will produce your personalized 1-Page Owner-Builder Plan as you read through each chapter and go through each stage of the process.

You will need to interact with organizations such as: real estate brokers and salespeople, mortgage advisors, lawyers, lenders, professional consultants, statutory bodies and all types of contractors. The 'Town Clerks' office will become an important destination. This is in addition to a combination of state, county, municipalities, townships, city, town, borough, village, province, regional municipality, local municipality, ville, arrondissement or unincorporated area offices and their local officials, all depending on which state or province you are in and the location of your lot.

> **TIP BOX**
>
> **Beware of the 'Savior Complex'**
>
> As a manager, you are striving to be everything to everybody and so far, things are going well. The project is making progress and people are impressed enough to let you get on with things and step back from getting in your way. Then you find that you are doing *everything* and not delegating. You are taking responsibility (good) but you are covering more and more items (not so good). It almost becomes accepted that you are the 'savior' and everything stops with you.
>
> This is not managing; this is total control, to the point where others have limited input. While it may be comforting to feel in total control, beware what you wish for. Teamwork is always better.

Many surveys identify people who accomplish more than the 'average', strive more than the average. To achieve something more than the average, for a while you too may have to work longer hours to get it done.

This book is set to challenge you and support you to achieve excellence.

I'm asking you to embrace and harness smart technology. To deliver this almighty project, you need to be organized and up for the challenge.

Don't worry if organization is not you! Rather than just thinking of what comes immediately next, The 1-Page Owner-Builder Plan encourages you to think ahead and see the big picture.

The big picture is the difference between a builder and an operative. A builder constructs with knowledge to a plan; an operative just operates on the next job as it presents itself.

Are You a 'Builder'?

A builder can see where he or she is and visualize where he wants to be. The builder will not know every answer at any point, but never fear, the tools and resources to deliver are available.

The builder will lead and inspire his team to become a 'crew' who are all working for each other. This aspect will call for leadership and constancy, and a good crew will give you loyalty and backup.

Or, Are You an 'Operative'?

The operative will plod on, operating pretty much in the dark and dealing with issues as they arise.

Will the operative's method be more expensive? – probably.

Will the operative work out of sequence? – definitely.

The operative may well succeed in the end. It's just that the end will be down a longer and more winding road.

With that in mind, let's make some real commitments.

- Time will be tight and your priorities will be questioned, so think them through
- High levels of physical and mental energy are required
- Be prepared to change your path if research turns up unexpected answers
- Constructing in the 'right way' is the best way
- Take pride in what you and your team do

This book aims to assist you by forewarning you… not having to only learn by your mistakes. Failing forward is a valid method of education, but you can also learn from *my* mistakes.

> **TRUE STORY**
>
> Matthew Daniels was a man with a mission – his aim was to run 535 half marathons on consecutive days – 7 days a week! He achieved this exceptional feat and listed the five key objectives he adopted to get through this ordeal. These objectives could have been written for the owner-builder.
>
> - Have a goal
> - Find a support network
> - Partners create accountability
> - Focus on the winning day
> - Overcome your obstacles

To aid your efficiency, I have produced a proposed outline 1-Page Owner Builder Plan. This is not meant to be your Owner-Builder Plan but more to show how it may look once you have started.

The build process is ongoing and never entirely complete until you sell up and leave the property. This is a good thing and this is a bad thing. It's good to have an interesting project giving you a lifetime of fun. It's a bad thing to have a project which you can never entirely finish!

The 1-Page Owner-Builder Plan indicates the various stages of the project and how you may break down the items in the 'big picture'. Throughout the chapters I have spread updated sample 1-Page Owner-Builder Plans that reflect issues that typically arise through the build process. These go into much more detail but are only for guidance. The point of the exercise is that you name your own headings and identify key points. This system will chart your course through the project. How much micro detail you go into is down to personal preference but it is important you feel confident that you know what is coming up. This assists you to recognize that you need further information on what is 'coming over the horizon'. The 1-Page Owner-Builder Plan should act as a prompter of what you need to address.

The idea is to break down tasks in a logical way and have an overall visual diagram of what needs to be done. When items are achieved, they can be highlighted or deleted, to be replaced by upcoming issues.

Introduction – Action

- Focus on your crew
- Confirm what you want to build, and where
- Start your 1-Page Build Plan

FIND PLOT
Contacts
Identify Area
6-Degrees of Separation
Auctions
Web Searches

TEAM
Set Up Files
Set Up File Sharing System
Family Support
Magazine Articles
Set Up Basic Accounts

IDENTIFY PLOT
Identify Designer
Outline Discussion When Possible plot(s) found
Site Visit
Site Assessment

MONEY
Calculate Wealth
Identify Leverage

COSTS
How much to purchase suitable finished home
Consider 'Unit Costs'

GENERAL
Go Home Different Routes To See What Is Being Built
Call Into Hardware Stores

CHAPTER 1
SUMMARY

Your new and emerging design can include many exciting developing technologies. By recognizing these pieces and bringing them together, you can complete the Jigsaw. This will assist discussions with your design team and move the project forward in a positive way, producing outstanding results.

Highlights covered by this chapter include:

- What Jigsaw picture are you creating?
- Do others understand what you tell them?
- It's the Environment, stupid
- Why is it important to build a 'Green House'?
- How large should your house be?
- Are 'Modern Methods of Construction' really modern?
- What can you do to promote wildlife at minimal cost?

CHAPTER 1

JIGSAW PUZZLE

A builders' protest march would see us all chanting: 'What do we want? GRADUAL CHANGE! When do we want it? IN DUE COURSE!'
— Kate Fox

What are you getting into? And will the timid steps of gradual change give way to radical change? Construction fashions and designs change slowly over many years and even when radical ideas come forward, the uptake can be slow when compared to other industries.

The jigsaw puzzle in this case is a fully blown 3-Dimensional object. It is a completed and fully functioning home you built and can enjoy. It is somewhere for your family to settle into and embrace. This is not for the faint hearted; this is serious business.

Completing the jigsaw is much more than fitting available 'pieces' in position. The pieces need to be designed, managed and created before they come together. And the pieces are not all tangible items. They also include planning, managing, and old-fashioned gut feeling that's linked to personal taste and experience.

The quality of the completed home is a major part of the puzzle. The structure must be sound and the quality of finish high. The strength of the structure will be set by building codes, to be checked by the building inspector. However, the quality of finish is a different matter altogether. Without a high quality finish, why bother?

Part of the puzzle is knowing which jigsaw picture you are completing. Before you can define what it is you want and move onto agreeing a working schedule with your professional team, you must consider the big picture: what you are designing and the grand vision to deliver the project.

Consider this:

- If you do not strive for a high quality finish
- If you do not strive for value for money
- If you do not want to build a specific property for your family needs
- If you do not want to have input into a thoughtful and efficient design
- If you do not want to build in high levels of energy efficiency
- If you do not wish to create something special and personal…

Save yourself lots of trouble and live in a house someone else constructed.

What are You Looking For?

The house should be pleasing to the eye and suit you and your partner's style. New houses can be difficult places for furniture from previous homes but you can enjoy the art of mixing and matching the old with the new. The home should be functional and efficient, and yet have personal spaces to pursue hobbies that the family enjoys. The kitchen as the engine room of the home is important and should be in touch with the other spaces.

How you achieve this and actually finish the project whilst remaining calm and collected is part of the bigger picture.

I recommend you employ design consultants and tradespeople to carry out works which cover skills you do not have or to keep scheduled progress up to date.

While viewing the design, you must have faith that the room sizes and heights will work for you. From their experience, designers can reassure you the spaces will work well, and they usually will. It's common for floor areas to look small during the construction process before walls are erected and ceiling heights to appear small after drywall sheets are fitted. Compare room dimensions in other buildings and discuss with your professionals and tradespeople. Too large a room can seem like a warehouse and too small can feel overcrowded and claustrophobic.

Communication at all levels is perhaps the greatest challenge. The designs need to be communicated to the planners, building professionals and local state or authority bodies. This is before the tradespeople and suppliers get involved and add their own interpretation.

It is often assumed, when outlining your needs, you have made yourself clear. You feel you could not have been more explicit. Others confirm they understand and are in agreement. An issue arises when this assumption is wrong and what you get is not what you (thought) you asked for.

TRUE STORY

I often make an apology to the listener who I am instructing on a specific point, after giving what I thought was clear and complete instruction. I say something like 'I am sorry to be a pain but just so it's said out loud …' I then go over the whole matter again, looking for input and confirmation from the listener. Have they really 'got it'?

Usually they have not 'got it' and we need to get right into it again to assure me our minds have met on what is being said. Sometimes, I am pleasantly reassured that all is well. Whatever the response, this approach has saved a lot of wasted energy and cost.

This does not mean the listener is not bright; simply, verbal communication is the least effective means of communication and you are expecting a lot from it!

I once saw a contractor instruct a worker to dig a foundation pit that was to be 20" (500mm) square x 39" (1.0m deep). He told the worker three things.

- The size of the hole to be excavated
- That he would return at 10:00am with the concrete
- Not to 'hang around' and to work hard

When the contractor returned that afternoon at 1pm, he was surprised to find the foundation 39" (1m) square x 60" (1.5m deep). This was frustrating for the contractor as he had to now remove 2 cubic yards (1.5 cubic meters) of spoil as opposed to 0.33 Cubic yards (0.25 cubic meters) and replace it with the increased amount of concrete (which he did not have with him). This was all unnecessary cost.

> Perhaps not unsurprisingly, the contractor enquired (quite forcibly) why the operative had over-dug the hole against his instructions. The worker replied that he had followed the instructions as he was told to work hard, and as instructed, he had kept on working. The worker reminded the contractor that he had said 'you did not want me hanging around'!
>
> The contractor thought he had given clear instructions and the operative thought he had followed them. If the contractor had issued a sketch or even cut a piece of timber to the appropriate length to act as a guide, this situation could probably have been avoided.

Who is to Blame?

It does not matter where blame lies, because as owner, in the end you always pay... in one way or another. Rather than worry about blame, expend your energy on clarity, how will you stop this type of thing re-occurring?

Provide anyone you instruct with designer's drawings, images, brochures, illustrations from building books... whatever it takes so there can be no misinterpretation of your design. What remains is your design and this is what you want implemented.

Sometimes a tradesperson will suggest a way of carrying out a task or finishing an item. They can be right, and their solution lies somewhere between acceptable and genius, but be wary. Sometimes it is just simply easier for them and less pleasing as a finish for you.

Employ professionals you feel you chime with. It is important to feel you can relate on a personal level with your design professionals. Do they share your vision and will they include you in the process? Will they get back to you with responses to your queries? Do you feel comfortable with the process? This is particularly important with key design professionals, who have the greatest input. If you are concerned, look further afield for professionals until all seems somehow right.

Can You Afford the Time it Takes to Owner-Build?

People often find the owner-build process becomes all-consuming. There are so many decisions to be made, right from the beginning. The designer will help but ultimately you need to be proactive. After work starts, the sheer number of decisions can be overwhelming. You either submit to the challenge and invest yourself completely … or you need to be very good at compartmentalizing.

Keeping Sane and Calm.

Organization and control of information is a large part of keeping stress levels in check. Consider now what you need to find out.

You know you want to construct a first class home which:

- Meets your current needs
- Allows for future expansion

You may not yet know:

- The design look, room layouts and functions of each area (but you know you want to build a home you can be proud of).
- Which skilled professionals or tradespeople you will employ or how they all fit into the schedule.
- How you will make yourself available for this responsibility if all other existing commitments are kept as they are.
- How much money you need to deliver your new home.
- How many decisions you will need to take and how many matters rely on other decisions.
- The importance of planning early and selecting furniture, finishes and equipment (FF&E) etc. ahead of time.
- How much stress building and finance matters may add to the ongoing stress in your world.
- The many times you will rely on good records and notes of conversations had with anyone and everyone.
- How important 'good' communication is! People must be crystal clear on what you want, or else you are failing to communicate.

Technologies and Modern Concerns You Should Generally Understand

You need a general understanding of a remarkably wide range of things when planning your house. It's practically a list of features of modern life. While it's not necessary to include each and every latest thing into your design, just be aware of them and have a general understanding of why they are current and how they may impact your life and future build. Consider the full gambit of what is available and whittle down decisions based on appropriateness, wish list, budget and design.

Different technologies and products are evolving all the time and what may seem irrelevant suddenly becomes relevant when longevity increases or simply the cost point comes down.

A few years ago, electric cars seemed to be reserved for the wealthy eccentric who did not mind delaying her journey several times a day to re-charge the battery and scrapping the car every three years (as this was its predicted lifespan). The world has since taken a turn, with dropping vehicle purchase costs, greater distance of travel without battery recharging, and a general disdain for fossil fuels. Today, electric cars are commonly accepted as the way forward for personal transportation.

It's the ENVIRONMENT, Stupid!

The environment is the new watchword and has become the single most fretted-over issue in design and construction. Regardless of your viewpoint over climate change or even if you have a 'nothing to see here, just move along please' point of view, it matters little, as all new properties are benchmarked against ever-increasing environmentally-friendly policies, with plenty of regulations advancing higher levels of energy efficiency. This includes both environmentally-friendly power generation and energy retention inside the home.

The good news is, as well as saving energy and using non-renewable resources, an environmentally-friendly attitude and operation will save you money. Some of the additions will immediately pay for themselves and some of them offer a relatively short payback period. The payback period is of course in direct correlation to how much the measures cost and where you are situated on the planet.

Environmental Management.

The way you manage the project on site directly affects the environment. If you carry out the work speedily, you will use less site energy. The lights are on and power is continuously used each week. The fewer weeks you are on site, the less general energy is used.

Tool Selection.

Battery tools are becoming the preferred choice for light work, while heavy duty electrical tools can be used in preference to diesel compressors powering mechanical equipment.

Waste Plan.

How are you going to dispose of the mountain of waste created by each and every construction project? Different types of waste can be separated and disposed of or recycled separately. Enquire with the waste removal companies what materials they prefer to be separated out. By complying, you can save the money they normally charge to separate. Many waste removal contractors prefer drywall sheet offcuts are separated and charge extortionately to accept mixed loads. Check preferences and save money.

Reduce Wasted Materials.

Extra materials are purchased as a normal part of the ordering process. Cuts from standard lengths will leave unusable pieces but how can you reduce this wasted material? Simple. Split orders down so that all the materials are not delivered at one time. This allows you to look at what materials are unused before your next order and reduce waste by fitting them into the works as opposed to discarding them.

By re-measuring as work proceeds, you can try to eliminate over-ordering and waste.

Plus, with careful planning, you can order a mixture of materials to make up a full delivery, which saves on vehicle journeys to your site from your supplier.

Re-use Materials Where You Can.

Store not-yet-used materials neatly on site and look out for opportunities to use materials from your on-site store, as opposed to always ordering new.

TRUE STORY

On a recent project we had to first carry out demolition work on an existing building before re-building could commence. By carefully taking down brick chimneys and external walls by hand as opposed to machine demolition, we were able to save, clean and stack piles of high quality second-hand stock bricks outside the construction area but still on the lot. We used these bricks to build boundary walls to the rear garden area.

This saved:

- Machinery hire costs, including machinery fuel
- Material removal costs
- Material disposal or recycling costs
- New material delivery costs
- New material costs
- A bonus of zero carbon footprint for delivery of materials

The look of the 'new' second-hand brickwork was magnificent and if we had purchased this quality of material, it would have blown the budget.

Eco-Friendly Building Design.

It's in your best interests to discuss ways that 'green' elements of design can be incorporated in the whole design, not merely as an add on to a non-green model. By following current regulations and improving on them where you can, your home will be built well and sustainably. You should incorporate current technology but allow space for upgrades to be installed as new technologies are introduced or existing technologies are improved. In practical terms, spaces are designed and voids allocated to later run new services and equipment. An element of flexibility is best run throughout the project.

Green Construction Practices.

The more people seek ways to reduce their carbon footprint and encourage a reduction of the carbon footprint of those around them, the more likely things are to change.

We can build responsibly by only purchasing raw materials from sustainable sources and by installing highly-insulated products, produced in a green environment.

Highlighting green production methods is becoming a badge of honor, with manufacturers pleased to take credit for their environmentally-aware processes. Green concerns are becoming a core issue at all parts of the supply chain.

Habitat.

We share a world with all types and sizes of insects, animals and birds yet it seems we are determined to occupy hermetically-sealed, creature-free homes. Perhaps leave a little bit of habitat so creatures can join us with somewhere to live. This can be achieved with relative ease and just a little thought.

You can incorporate creature-friendly features into the design. Consider turning your roof coverings into a meadow with sedum or grass or you can provide nesting places for birds by positioning 'bird bricks' high up in the structure or by fixing bird boxes to trees. The garden could have a pond to encourage frogs and also become an attractive water feature.

If all new homes had a garden pond, it would have a dramatic effect on habitat.

A complementary issue is what we can do differently to safeguard birds, including by designing in bird-friendly windows. According to the American Bird Conservancy, an estimated 1 billion birds are killed in the US each year by birds flying into glazed screens; for example, those around swimming pools and large windows. Lightly hanging, swaying cords or wires coming down over the windows can significantly reduce the number of bird strikes. These are cheap, simple options and can be seamlessly added. Glass designs can be a more intricate solution and with a little thought, an aesthetic one.

> **TIP BOX**
>
> Bird Friendly Legislation in New York City
>
> New York City Council decided bird-friendly buildings are the preferred option to protect wildlife in this most urban of environments. They are not only focussing on the large glass windows which cause havoc to the bird population but on appropriate lighting and heating as part of their bird friendly strategies. One such effort to incorporate designs to facilitate bird safety was displayed well in an upgrade to the Jacob K. Javits Convention Center. They since reported a reduction of birds dying by 90%. This could be something which will be adopted internationally.

> The point is, one of the reasons for owner-building is it provides you with opportunities to *upgrade* your design beyond the norm.

External Lighting.

External lighting is an area where a little thought and hardly any effort can make a huge difference to your average moth. Moths pollinate plants and are a food source for birds, bats, lizards and other insects. Their numbers are dramatically dropping because of external lighting. These lights, usually incandescent lamps, are fatal for the moth and other bugs and are killing them off in worrying numbers.

Artificial lighting is also a problem for wildlife, as the night sky is illuminated by street lights, house lights, dawn to dusk security lights, motion sensor lights, car lights and other lights. You will be adding to this with external lights, and so what kind of lights should we install and how should they be positioned?

Down Facing Lamp

Bug Friendly.

Yellow/Orange/Warm hue LED lights are shown by research to be most moth and bug friendly. These are even better than some light fittings advertised as serving this purpose and LED lighting consumes significantly less energy.

Kelvins are measurements of heat. The symbol for a Kelvin is 'K'.

The less heat measured, the warmer the color of an LED lamp. So, if you want a *'warm white* light', you should install a lamp below 3,500K. *Cool white* is between 6–7,000K, while a daylight, or natural light, is 10,000K.

What the light is used for will ultimately decide which *type* of light is selected. Cool white light is most suitable for areas requiring concentration and this is ramped up to daylight or natural light. Warmer light is used for relaxation areas and where a feeling of ambience is wanted.

> **TIP BOX**
>
> The four main reasons for external lighting is:
>
> - *Navigation* – Can you safely access your house?
> - *Security* – Does night time lighting increase safety or just give criminals improved vision?
> - *Aesthetics* – Do you wish to illuminate certain features of the home?
> - *Entertaining* – Do you entertain in external areas after dark?
>
> By all means, have external lighting for the above reasons, just design your lighting so it's bug friendly and does not pollute the heavens.

Sizing of Structural Members.

Over-sizing structural members (beams & columns) is a tricky subject. You are reliant on your designer and structural engineer to offer their best advice and to design efficiently. 'Overdesign' aka 'over-engineering' is a term used to describe a product or part that can perform to a level higher than is required. This increases the use of materials, costs more to purchase, and ecologically has a greater impact on our environment. Every engineer will assure you they are miserly when it comes to design sizes, but research shows many structural supports can take much higher loads than are imposed. The Structural Engineers Association of California (SEAOC) found that "strength design procedures…. can result in significantly more efficient use of materials". This can substantially cut carbon emissions in steel manufacturing. All you can do is question designs and encourage your engineer to specify smaller structural members, remembering that safety must come first and compliance is essential.

Use Buildings Smartly.

One issue not often discussed is how actual-user habits in many sustainably-designed buildings differ to their planned efficiencies. The US Green Building Council (USGBC) reports there can be as much as a 250-percent performance gap between design levels and actual performance.

Is this all due to poor installation or is the cause as likely to be the way the buildings are used?! Living in the home, users have a responsibility to act in a green-conscious way to get the best results. In many cases, they are not nearly as efficient as they can be. Even in the best-case scenarios, the performance gap has been found to be 80-percent below optimum design level. So, don't only design smart buildings – use buildings smartly!

Tiny House.

Many people believe the modern, large and generally getting larger house is not environmentally-sustainable and is increasingly less affordable. This is before you get started on accounting for ongoing running and fossil fuel costs.

An answer touted of late is having a traditional house but on a much, much smaller scale. In this spirit, you simply do not hoard or buy stuff which will not fit into your tiny space. If you are not naturally neat, you will need to learn to become neat or the Tiny House is not for you.

Many cities have zoning laws that will not allow such small homes and require minimum space standards are met as well as minimum lot and density size. 'Tiny House' has however become a movement and may well pop up as 'bridge' housing for people seeking permanent homes. In some cities they are permitted as accessory dwelling units (ADU's) that are positioned beside traditional homes for family member use.

Modern Methods of Construction (MMC)

Every few years, something comes along and is hailed as a modern (and better) method of construction. This has been the case for computerization of the home incorporating levels of artificial intelligence (AI) and automation. These are certainly advancing how we live in our homes and how hard our homes work to make our life a little easier. Nonetheless, a truly modern method of construction is quite a claim. Every method of construction I am aware of has been around for many millennia. Using timber to build homes is not new and neither is brick, concrete or straw. That said, there have been advances in materials or new uses.

Factory production of items such as laminated wooden beams has led to larger spans without central columns or support. Steel has been used very effectively in modern homes too. Sheet materials of many kinds are used as support, such as in flooring or in finish, with grained wood and plastic becoming a finish look in bathrooms and kitchens. Externally concrete and aerated blocks, with insulation materials factory-attached, has radically changed the world of traditional brickwork.

In fact, there have been changes throughout the years. Cavities in external walls started in Europe in the 19th century and cross-wall construction designs from the 1950s, allowing terraces to be built with support shared across different homes aided high density developments. Sears, Roebuck and Co. sold kit houses between 1908 and 1942 with 370 different designs; kits had timbers pre-cut to length. Over 70,000 were sold throughout the US and Canada. Portable cabins have been used commercially for offices, schools, canteens and hospitals for many years. Every construction site seems to grow a number of cabins for temporary offices and on-site facilities.

In the 1960s, walls and windows were constructed and put together off-site and slotted together to make tower blocks many stories high. This was efficient and cheap and, it transpired, inherently dangerous with resulting high-rise structural failure and collapse.

So, what allows enthusiasts to claim that off-site construction is now a Modern Method of Construction, or MMC? What has changed is how they are put together off-site and delivered to site.

The bringing together of Artificial Intelligence (AI), Computer Aided Design (CAD), Building Information Management (BIM), Virtual Reality (VR), Augmented Reality (AR), robotics, 3 dimensional (3D) printing, volumetric/modular construction and off-site factories have now changed the game sufficiently to bring this to a point where it can credibly be claimed the future will be a very different place for the homebuilder. A name has been given to this coming together, the 4th Industrial Revolution (4IR) of all these technologies that are collectively changing how we live in this world and how we react with technology. This has led onto Parametric design, with optimising design goals for the house which are taken from a set of constraints. If you want your room larger, the design software will calculate and design and determine what all the implications of this simple change will be. It will change the lengths of beams and reschedule materials that would have previously been the subject of a lot of detailed design by expensive consultants.

Definitions and Explanations.

Artificial Intelligence (AI) is intelligence demonstrated by machines with a level of reasoning or knowledge. This often allows objects to be manipulated or moved.

Computer Aided Design (CAD) creates sophisticated technical drawings. The system can calculate areas and produce different versions from information stored within the program. These can be manipulated to create elevations from plans and produce many levels of information within a single drawing.

Building Information Management (BIM) builds on the CAD process and all the designers work off the same base 'drawing' adding layers and levels of information ensuring full information sharing across all disciplines.

Virtual Reality (VR) is a simulated feeling and look of what something would be like but completely based on virtual information. You can, through a VR headset, feel you are walking through a completed property and view finishes before it is even constructed.

Augmented Reality (AR) is often confused with VR, although the key difference is that the computer-generated information enhances perception of reality and is not completely based on virtual information.

Robotics is the development of machines which replicates human actions and can carry out specific repetitive or directed tasks. This technology can be utilized effectively when fabricating homes within a factory environment. On-site robotics have been trialled around the world; in fact, robot-only roadbuilding was reported in China, but this technology is yet to make an impact on mainstream construction sites.

3D Printing is a term covering many different processes, with material layered into three dimensional objects. In construction, this raw material can be plastics or concrete, with researchers printing experimental concrete homes and bridges.

Volumetric/Modular construction means connecting pre-finished modules to make a whole room or indeed a whole house. These pieces may need covering with an external finish or may be completed with pre-made modular pieces. It will generally be placed onto a traditionally prepared foundation and concrete slab.

A Vision for the Future of Building.

Successful trials of 3D printing of concrete is ongoing in research and design (R&D) environments. Others have re-created many everyday products, for example making 'plastic bricks' out of household waste by printing strips of plastic and weaving them into brick shapes.

Innovation will impact on which materials are selected and how new buildings are constructed.

Gradual change may well give way to fundamental change; these new methods and materials will impact how design professionals interact and how a building is constructed. This will bring in radical movements up and down the whole supply chain. Other industries are moving ahead with this technology, including 3D printing within aircraft and car production.

With the latest apps for video group meetings and remote discussions at most people's fingertips, there's less need to travel to site. Project data and 3D models can all be group shared and many are now finding that higher productivity results from virtual meetings.

Generally, the off-site construction world wants the builder to provide a concrete slab and infrastructure services. On top of this very accurately placed slab and services will be your perfectly positioned and high-functioning factory-built house. You could liken this method to a car plant producing car models with specific engine design ranges but with various optional external features.

They deliver either components or pods that are constructed off-site. These are pre-finished wall or façade panels or specific rooms such as bathrooms and kitchens. They can be manufactured and delivered, to be installed complete.

For the owner-builder tempted by this construction method, you can never be too early in planning and concept because a traditionally-designed house might not be effectively adapted to MMC. The solutions and designs will be different to normal, and if you had already achieved a planning consent you would likely need to submit an entirely new application. The good news would be that the planners had already accepted the principle of residential construction on your lot and the overall bulk and heights of the structure set.

Your MMC designer can be the same person as your traditional house designer. She will interreact with the off-site contractor or you can engage directly with the 'outreach design professionals' who are the designers employed directly by the manufacturer. They know the products and can design around what is offered by the manufacturer.

The design must comply with the manufacturer's system and the home will be produced within their dry, hygienic and well-run factory. It will have high levels of OH&S, production slots, just-in-time management, robotic production methods and all it encompasses. It will be digitally 'Designed for Manufacture and Assembly' (DFMA) and assembled to a tolerance of 1/4" (6mm). With manufacturing records accurately kept, future maintenance and repair can be carried out in the knowledge of what is where.

The items often subject to DFMA are:-

- Wall Panels
- Floor Cassettes
- Façade Panels
- Columns & Beams
- Bathrooms
- Kitchens

Tolerances.

All the drainage, electrical, water services, etc. must be installed within or under your slab, and it's best if connections by the utility companies are prearranged so you can move in without delay. On-site tolerances for your slab and services will be advised by the manufacturer but may well be with +/- ¼" (6mm).

Cross Laminated Timber (CLT).

CLT is a process of engineering wood into a product from which the entire home can be constructed. Thin layers of wood (lamellas) are bonded together at alternating angles running the grain at a 90 degree angle to the lamination above and below. This makes a very strong and flexible material. CLT panels are suitable for the production of floors, walls and roofs. These can be formed as pre-insulated units and shipped to site for erection. CLT is a thought provoking material of the future that can provide exciting spaces and very interesting architecture.

Finishes.

You'll do the whole design and selection of finishes much earlier than in a traditional build as it must be fixed and frozen before manufacture commences. The tiles are specifically ordered, as are the kitchen units, and every handle and screw is specified before anything at all is produced. All lighting points, power points, telephone points, TV cables and satellite dishes are placed in pre-fixed positions and hardwired in. Manufacturers produce phone apps listing 'their' component parts and the designs evolve around their standard fittings. They will produce a 'kit of parts' (KoP) which will be installed at their works or attached and sent to site for fitting. In their world, they are working towards all onsite works to be relatively unskilled and as labor- free as they can. They want the technical delivery in their factory and the actual construction process to resemble flat pack furniture assembly that is put together with a screw driver and an 'Allen' or hex key.

This does not mean all the houses look the same; the pods are just designed and built around their standards and offered finishes. A house constructed within this system may look nothing like the one following it off the assembly line.

A real concern is your site's suitability for cranes and forklifts, along with questions of possible road closures for deliveries from factory to site. The off-site builder needs to be able to deliver the units safely and the space on site to install them.

Can manufacturers offer their services to produce single homes? This is a point to check with potential suppliers. Some manufacturers claim a home can be commenced, constructed and erected within 10 weeks, though I expect more complicated custom build homes to take longer.

The off-site manufacturers do claim faster design and construction times, reduced costs, sustainable solutions and fewer defects but you are buying into their 'kit of parts'.

A further issue is compliance bodies. The manufacturers claim the homes will easily last the minimum 60 years required by certification bodies and well beyond. There are already certifying insurance schemes with sufficient coverage for mortgages to be granted to new buyers. Check with all the bodies and lenders in your region to ensure specific schemes comply and your home will be authorized as suitable for you to lend on. Also check there is approval for you to sell on your property at some future point and a future purchaser can also reasonably lend against the property to allow them to purchase.

Funding.

Off-site manufacturers have a different take than traditional builders as far as valuations and funding is concerned. As they are manufacturing for you, they require substantial deposits and payments before and during manufacture and before delivery. This is totally different to the traditional valuation methods understood by mainstream lenders.

2030 & 2050.

All over the world governments seem to be projecting that real change will occur by either 2030 or 2050. Just far enough into the future to direct the ship of state but not too close to effect short term concerns of national current affairs. The UN is calling for all countries to commit to meeting net zero emission targets. Most countries are making commitments and are tightening up codes and standards to promote technologies to deliver on this aspiration. Manufacturers are listening to their governments and to the national governments of their major export markets and do not want to be left behind when new products or lower emission standards are introduced. This encourages invention and technical development and many believe the process will speed up at a faster rate than anticipated. This is all speculation but reinforces the point of you adopting high insulation levels and reducing energy consumption as part of your new home.

According to National Grid ESO fundamental change will be needed to meet the climate change challenge by 2050. Their Future Energy Scenario (FES) foresees major changes to transport, heating and energy efficiency. They believe that the pathway for a 'normal' residential house will have the following as standard:-

- High levels of insulation
- Elimination of unplanned ventilation
- Smart meter
- Electric hob & oven

- Smart hybrid heat pump
- All appliances are smart and A++++
- Home energy management system (HEMS)
- Battery storage in house
- 1 electric vehicle (EV) charge point
- Triple glazed windows
- PV solar panels on roof
- Bicycle space (together with a bicycle that is regularly used)

They are looking to a future where houses use 70% less energy than today and this is a good checklist to benchmark your thoughts against their predictions. All new homes are to be ultra-efficient.

What will this New World Look Like?

Very similar to the one we live in today as the current or legacy stock of houses will still be in place. New homes will change in appearance as their energy performance levels improve. Energy use will dip in response to ever efficient technological advances. The natural world may well appear closer with the realisation of the benefits of shrubs and ponds to the environment and the designing in of creature friendly features.

Prosumers.

Consumers who proactively seek out smart technologies and PV systems etc. are termed 'prosumers'. The energy companies believe that the prosumer is an evolving pressure group made up of people who will push for energy efficiency and produce their own renewable energy. Flexibility of supply to the grid by the widespread use of smart appliances and electric vehicles will reduce the reliance on traditional energy generation. A home energy management system (HEMS) will automatically select when appliances should be turned on or off to benefit the consumer by taking advantage of cheaper tariffs. It is thought that the introduction of HEMS will promote the rise of the prosumer. If you feel you may be open to maximising the FES challenge perhaps you should seriously look at embracing the Passive House approach.

Complete the Jigsaw.

To complete the jigsaw where all the pieces are not tangible or visible - is quite a difficult concept. There are lots of 'moving parts' and each detail is important and impacts the finished standards. You must be aware throughout the project of your destination, your vision, and have a plan to get there.

Do not under-estimate the importance of cost management! Sniff out value wherever you can. Those extra savings can make all the difference on completion. By carefully monitoring the home throughout the build you can follow up and record progress and miracle of miracles complete on time and on budget. The physical home is on hand as a testament to show you delivered the project.

Chapter 1 – Action Points

- What technologies are you interested in researching?
- How will modern technology enter your design process?
- Consider your FES and if Passive House is right for you?

CHAPTER 2
SUMMARY

What do you need to consider when reviewing a lot? You need to be sure that this is the right one and will work well for you. You must think like a developer and see how improvements can be made.

Interesting things covered by this chapter include:

- Zoning ordinances and permits
- Build permits
- Development and subdivision
- Types of lots
- Density of developments
- Lots change over the seasons
- What is 'Hope Value'?

CHAPTER 2

ASSESSING YOUR LOT

'Buy land, they're not making it anymore'.
– Mark Twain

Lot Finding

Realtors list local vacant land for sale and real estate websites promote land and building lots covering regions across Canada and the US. Realtors have a 'multiple listing service' (MLS), which is a subscription service that is state/county specific and they can also see if any lenders have a restriction over the property or if the land is mortgage-free. If you are interested in a particular property not currently listed for sale, you may be able to track down the owner by researching the property on lists maintained in the local Town Clerks Office or publicly available county records of properties. This information may be available online. This can be a quick and cheap resource of information.

The search usually starts off with an idea of what you are looking for, but as you view and reject lots, you narrow down what it is you are actually after. You start to appreciate that, with imagination, lots which initially appear unsuitable could work very well. The more you look at lots and vacant land, the more you'll notice what others have built. And you'll form opinions of what you *do not like* as much as what you do.

In highly-populated areas, many sites which would formerly not have been viable and valuable have become so. Both inner city and pristine rural areas have often risen in value well above rates of inflation. So, you must be alive to opportunities and have vision to see prospects where perhaps others have not.

Never dismiss personal contacts; do you know someone who knows of a great spot? Capitalize on the six degrees of separation phenomenon and let folks on social media know what it is you are looking for. A friend of a friend of a friend may well be able to help.

> **TRUE STORY**
>
> I was shown a social media message by my daughter from one of her long-time friends from school. It was asking if anyone knew of an apartment for sale at a certain price level in a city area. My daughter was just showing me this as part of a conversation on how wild apartment prices have become. I actually had an apartment I was thinking of putting on the market and so, prompted by this, we contacted her friend. Not long later, the deal was done. As we did not use a realtor, we had nil marketing fees and a discount was given!
>
> My daughter's friend knew vaguely I was in property but had not even considered approaching me. This was a social media message paying off.

If you have an idea of your budget to purchase a lot, increase your scope to include lots somewhat above your financial limit. Sometimes, just sometimes, a seller can be open to offers. People have all sorts of demands on them and a probing discussion can bring forward negotiation and all sorts of deals. It is not a good idea to spend above available funds but try to get the price reduced to meet the budget.

> **TIP BOX**
> Online property listings are often filtered to view by grouping available lots together in rising monetary values of say $10K. So if you are looking to purchase for say $200K, seek properties above this limit, as otherwise they may not be shown by the search engine.

How is Real Estate Described and Measured?

Across North America there are four standard descriptions of real estate.

- Lot and Block (recorded on plat drawings). This is a system based on subdivided plans already registered and accepted. Your lot will be designated by its county, lot and block number and plat number.

- Rectangular (government) survey. The land was divided into large rectangles that are referenced by principal meridians and base lines. There are only 37 meridians running from north to south across the whole of North America. This indicates the large areas covered. They are broken down again and again in regular shapes until they get to your lot.
- Metes and Bounds. This is the oldest system, going back to the settlement of the US before the American Revolutionary War. Markers and physical features record the boundaries of the property.
- Torrens Certificate (10 US states only). This is a system where the holder of a Torrens certificate is assigned full ownership.

Each type of description may be independent of each other or are sometimes combined. Modern technology is coming into play and geographic information systems (GIS) - which is a satellite based information system provides accurate data. Basically, you must accept local custom as you have no alternative.

Six degrees of separation

Are You a Developer?

In the purest sense, a developer is someone who acquires land, then develops and transforms it into a personalized home. This can be a vacant lot, one with a current residential use or one with a current non-residential use.

Your Lot.

Once you have identified 'your' lot as the one you wish to purchase, you must confirm to yourself that it's a good choice. Do not consider proceeding to a legally-binding contract before you are absolutely sure of what you are doing. When you are sure, contact a lawyer and check the contract and associated matters. Do not commit to purchase if issues are outstanding or need clarification.

Get an Opinion.

Visit the lot with your designers for their view on the potential of you building 'your home' on this lot. They will offer an independent take on the suitability of the site and perhaps see positives and negatives you have not considered. The designer will be very interested in the location of the property as this will determine local controls set by your zone. Together with your designer you will consider what direction the home would face and how this works with the sun's orientation during different times of the day and during each season. This will affect the layout of daytime living areas in your home. They will look for a clear view of *solar* (geographic) *south* to weigh up the available benefits of renewable solar energy and also consider the natural features and contours of the lot. Think through access and egress to the site and the city or towns view on allowing vehicle access or what car parking spaces you must provide. Points and deliberations over tree coverage and previous uses of the land along with evidence of local and existing services will be considered at some length.

In wildfire-prone regions you must confirm with your local planners that you are allowed to develop a house on the lot. All other signs could be that you are zoned properly and can easily get a building permit and other neighboring houses have been built. Yet the last few years have seen massive wildfires and local attitudes to fire safety can quickly change. Do not be the last person to know, and be left with a lot that cannot be built on. To be a cautious purchaser you can discuss this with the fire officer and get a fire rating issued prior to purchase.

Each lot needs careful consideration. An area on high ground can look wonderful in the summer months but be treacherous from wind and snow during other seasons. Equally, low lying land can turn into a bog or be covered by water at different times of the year. Look at any site-specific issues with fresh eyes and see how your lot may be affected. Check if the area is subject to flooding, wildfires, snow storms, hurricanes, is located in the 'tornado belt' or any other natural or becoming more prevalent feature. The onset of climate change has made us reassess how we look at house locations and the natural surroundings we set them in. In all likelihood you already live in the area you wish to build your new home and so you'll be aware of general conditions. If the location is good, when you come up with a unique solution to develop the lot, the building of your home becomes exhilarating.

I personally do not like to look for inspiration in design books of plans or 'packages' to find a solution to the question of what to build. The designs offered can seem a speedy and complete option, offering a standard and safe approach, however, they are a predetermined packaged solution that is not specially made to suit your family and your life.

Many people, however, are attracted to the idea of a design and build company who will almost take over and deliver a completed project. This will be in line with their 'house style'. These companies give you the boost of fixing your budget, with extra work priced in before you instruct. They often have *show homes* you can inspect to 'visualize' your house before it's started. This approach is popular with lenders as they then take the risk of your performance as a builder out of the equation.

Terms.

Terms widely used to describe types of land or describing what has happened to the terrain:

Previously Developed Land.

Land that was previously built upon and in all likelihood is not contaminated. Perhaps underground structural walls, foundations or basements are still in place. There are no guarantees and caution should always be exercised.

Brownfield Land.

Land previously used for industrial or commercial purposes is known as a 'brownfield' site if real or perceived contamination exists. The important point is that the previous use may well have contaminated the land with toxic wastes. These can be overcome but they have a cost to do so. To encourage brownfield sites to be taken back into use, The *Small Business Liability Relief and Brownfields Revitalization Act* (Brownfields Law) became law in the US in 2002. Property developers (owner-builders) who are cleaning up a site (known as remediation) and who are not responsible for the on-site toxic waste which they did not contribute to or cause are sometimes shielded from the cost of the cleanup. However, the owner-builder may have to pay the full cost of the remediation works needed if the purchase price was reduced to reflect the cost of repairing the contamination.

The Canadian Brownfields Network (CBN) currently campaigns for a cleanup across all of Canada and so each province has a introduced a series of initiatives and laws for their areas. As with everything legal, be cautious and take specific expert advice if you are developing a brownfield site.

Greenfield Land.

Land which has never been built on or used for other than general agricultural purposes, is known as a 'greenfield' lot. Be cautious; just because a parcel of land has not been previously developed, it does not mean that previous uses have not left their mark. Are there filled-in dams or water holes for agronomical uses, that were considered normal back in previous centuries? Remnants of agricultural wells or buildings may still be in place.

Hill House

Flood Plain.

An area prone, not necessarily annually, but historically, to flooding. They are often near bodies of water, such as rivers or lakes.

Earth Sheltered.

A lot developed to partially cover the house from view, topped with retaining earth. This works well where there is a natural feature of a hill or cliff on the property which the house can be 'snuggled' into. Earth sheltering is also a highly efficient way to insulate a property and can offer protection from wildfires and other natural weather occurrences.

Underground.

A house built out of view by dropping the level of the property under the natural height and contours of the lot. The house can be completely covered or appears to be so from a distance. The site retains its natural look as unbuilt land. In certain climates, homes are constructed like this to mitigate extreme weather temperatures or to allow a building to be constructed which does not impact the landscape.

Cut-in Sites.

Lots on a natural slope or on a hill. It can be more cost-effective to step the house down in line with the slope as opposed to 'digging in'. This can make for interesting split-level features while keeping the house height in line with a set distance above local ground-level.

Land Reclamation.

Lands recovered from existing bogs, seas, riverbeds, etc. are called reclaimed land. This can be a very expensive process, but when location is key it can be deemed worthwhile on a cost analysis basis.

Land Rehabilitation.

Land is returned through remediation of contaminants to a previous state, having suffered damage from an industrial contamination or farming purpose. For example, old waste dumps used for landfills or agricultural dams that are drained and refilled with solid materials. Careful advice should be sought where residential land is offered for sale in these cases, as gas build-ups and subsidence can occur if the works were not scrupulously specified and carried out.

Restricted and Unrestricted Land.

In some states land is listed as unrestricted or has 'zero' planning or applicable zoning ordinances. This means the land has no pre-set use associated with it. This is as opposed to restricted land, which is zoned for a specific use or purpose.

This can be exciting, as you can apply for a new permission (called variances) for almost anything, but it does not mean you will be successful; it's just that you will not be bound by a previous or specific use. Zoning regulations can still apply, as can restrictions from other sources such as easements, rights-of-way, or deeds.

One thing to bear in mind is: if your land is unrestricted perhaps your neighbor's land is as well. If you object to your neighbor's proposed use, you may not be able to use the 'existing use' argument to stop or alter their development. You should seek guidance from a planning consultant on all planning matters, as detail is all in this world.

> **TIP BOX**
>
> Soil Tests
>
> If the plot is unable to have a direct public sewer connection you will need to consider a septic water treatment system. A licensed soil scientist or engineer will carry out a 'Perc' (percolation) test to determine the percolation rate of the soil and evaluate the suitability of the land for a septic system. These results will be the basis for the design of a suitable system, at your location. This information can be important when creating build-cost budgets as higher soil resistance results in a higher system cost. It is a serious step to spend money hiring consultants for tests on a property you do not own. This needs to be balanced against the potential cost of a poor percolating soil test result after purchase.
>
> The soil suitability is also a matter of concern as the soil condition determine the size and depth of the foundations. Your engineer will be able to advise you.
>
> Always ask the seller if they have information on the ground conditions and if they do, will they pass over a copy so that you can get an opinion from your consultants? It may be that a seller will commission tests to assure you that the lot is a good purchase.

Zoning.

The federal government's and states/provinces do not have zoning ordinances, rather this is left to local communities. Any influence they have is through environmental laws, coastal or State Parks and National Parks' management, and scenic easements and restrictions.

Local government and municipalities want orderly and planned growth that fits with their view of the world. They like to have housing areas, industrial areas, shops and commercial areas all neatly placed in locations to meet their masterplan. To this end they developed zones, within zones, and subdivided plots to meet the desired outcome. They achieved this through the development of a 'local comprehensive plan'.

These are established through powers delegated by central government, who in turn enable acts and pass these onto counties and local municipalities.

A city will usually have many different zoning districts and each district will be subject to their own local regulations or ordinances. Zone ordinances can often dictate design by introducing policies that the representatives of the local town wish to enforce.

Life does not always fit into such tidy 'boxes'. Many buildings and uses pre-date the zones and rely on 'grandfathered' permissions to remain.

Developers often push back at the designations and stipulated restrictions particularly in urban areas where many mixed uses exist next to each other. This is also the case in rural locations, where residential developments can be rare. This rareness increases their value. Planned unit developments and subdivisions often have restrictions placed on design and building development by residential community associations or by a deed. These can be restrictive and stop you having a free hand in matters of design, height, lot coverage and location of your home with regard to other homes or allowable property setbacks (the distance that structures and/or paving must be from a boundary). Other restrictions and covenants can become apparent on closer examination.

Sometimes it makes sense to seek to work within the scheduled zones and sometimes it serves you well to work outside of the system and seek a change-of-use or variance in order to get the permission you want.

This is of course subjective, so from the very beginning be cautious and seek out and follow professional planning advice at every stage.

Zoning effects what can be constructed and where, the following points are typically considered:

- Permitted use
- Land parcel sizes
- Category of allowable structures
- Care, conservation and protection of the environment
- Property line setbacks
- Development density
- Roof and roof fixed plant heights from local levels
- Protection of nature and natural resources
- Percentage of land coverage by impervious surfaces
- External appearances and styles
- Employment protection

The locally agreed plan is produced to serve the community and does this best when it contributes to sustainable development. The local people in the main have some idea of how they would like their home area to be developed and what features they would like to be preserved or changed. Often locals just like things to remain as they are. The local municipality and the elected representatives like to stand up for local feelings and are often elected on this remit. So, this is where planning becomes a balance of retaining the old and melding in the new.

What is the Permit Status?

Developments are mainly subject to two different codes: the Building Code and the Zoning Ordinance. From these codes the two key documents needed are a Zoning Permit and a Building permit.

Usually the Zoning Permit is required prior to the issue of a building permit, towns and cities often have alternative approaches based on the actual project. Some projects are given zone clearance during the Building Permit process and other projects require a separate Zoning Permit before moving onto the Building Permit application.

When a separate Zoning Permit is required prior to making the Building Permit application, this will usually entail a full submission of site layouts and sometimes building plans. Other codes (fire codes etc.) may also need to be addressed at this stage of the application.

Canadian provinces may require that you seek a development permit before a building permit can be applied for. This is a permit issued to cover any change of use to the land that will be required for your 'development' to proceed. This is regulated by their Zoning and Development By-laws.

Do not take the word of anyone involved in marketing the site. You need to confirm the permit status yourself because from this point onwards, you are liable to pay for the associated fees and incurred expenses. To help you, the planning history is often freely available on the local town planning website.

Zoning Permit.

The issue of a zoning permit confirms that your proposed use meets the approved development types scheduled within your lot's specific zoning district or zoning ordinance. This is all well and good if it fits within the ordinance framework, but if the land or building does not currently conform with the zoning ordinance, you must establish that you can either continue the nonconforming use or that your new development will be allowed to continue with this nonconforming use. Do not make assumptions that you consider 'reasonable'; remember, clarity and confirmation is always better. In many cases a current nonconforming use is not approved if the existing structure is demolished or substantially amended. You may well have to seek a conditional-use permit (special use permit) to continue the use.

A petition can be submitted to a zoning hearing board (or zoning board of appeals) for exceptions from the zoning ordinance and you can seek a conditional use permit or a variance to allow your development and ongoing use.

The other way forward is for a property owner to seek to alter the current zoning classification by amending the zoning ordinance or the district map. This will commence a complicated and expensive process involving layers of local government. Perhaps not a route for the faint hearted but a possibility. If you are not sure over any zoning issue, contact the planners or get advice from a professional planning consultant.

In line with local practice, you may well next have to apply for a Building Permit. This permit is only issued if your construction proposals meet with the building codes. The majority of jurisdictions in the US have adopted the International Building Code (IBC) and the International Residential Code (IRC) and in Canada the National Building Code (NBC). Each province and state can choose to adopt the codes in full or partially. Florida for example has a statewide building control regime to meet concerns over hurricanes while 'The Ontario Fire Code' varies significantly from the Canadian 'National Fire Code'. State and provincial governments delegate control and enforcement to cities and townships.

Both zoning appeals and building permit appeals are directed locally. They can be the responsibility of the local municipal body or are heard by a city wide-board. Check your position locally.

Current/Elapsed Permits.

Building Permits are usually issued for a stated period. Some areas set a time limit by which the application must be commenced, in others it is set to when the project must be complete. If the permit is not enacted by that date, it automatically elapses. You must assure yourself an elapsed permit can be reinstated.

Historic Conservation or Preservation.

Some areas are listed and recognized as historic and worthy of conservation. These are specified zones where existing structures are to be maintained and therefore proposals are considered alongside official guidelines to preserve and protect the historic nature of the area. Often features will need to be added and special care taken before a permit is issued. A conversation will be necessary to discern whether the point is to conserve the area by having minimal visible change from how it currently is… or is the intent of the regulations aimed at returning the area to a previous era? Is there any place for new buildings that keep the area special with sensitive design options?

Historic conservation/preservation consultants often work alongside local historic conservation groups and advise these groups on applications and general advice on the appropriateness of applications. It is not difficult to find out who advises these groups locally as it is usually common knowledge and they appear at meetings and advise committees. It can be worthwhile discussing your plans with these consultants and even requesting that they act on your behalf. This is in no way improper as they are recognized as having expertise in your local town and understand the dynamics of the area. They will publicly state that they have an interest in the project and proper divisions of confidentiality will be made to maintain the local democratic process.

Local Permit Requirements.

Provinces, states, cities and towns have local permit regulations that you must make yourself aware of and comply with. The Canadian City of Vancouver is typical and a selection of the following permits will be required dependant on the work you are undertaking:

- Building permit
- Demolition permit
- Development permit
- Electrical permit
- Fire hydrant use permit
- Fire sprinkler permit
- Noise exception permit
- Occupancy permit
- Operating permit
- Plumbing and gas permits
- Solar photovoltaic (PV) panels permit
- Tree removal permit
- Underground storage tank or abandonment permit
- Wastewater discharge permit
- Water and sewer connection permit

Some of these permits will be self or specialist contractor certified and some will require an on-site inspection. As ever you must check out the requirements for your project.

Potential.

Realtors often term properties for sale as 'having potential' subject to the issue of necessary zoning and building permits. This means the site does not have a building permit, but perhaps you can achieve one. All permit applications carry the risk of refusal.

The question is: why *does it not have a planning permit in place?*

This would make it a higher value asset?

If the owner *had* applied and received permission, it would increase his value and sale price.

Perhaps an application was submitted and later withdrawn?

Did the owner seek permission and was refused… or is 'hope value' a part of the sale price?

It is worth asking yourself if the land is offered for sale on the basis of its perceived value?

Is the price in line with its current planning permission?

If you do think this, does the land have a higher potential value if an enhanced permission was sought and gained?

Hope Value.

'Hope value' is a higher valuation for a lot than is deserved in current condition or with current zoning or planning status. The purchaser 'hopes' to achieve an improved planning permission and is prepared to back this belief with hard cash. They will offer more than the current land value as they expect to receive a higher return on delivery of the better permission. This sounds doubtful, but it is a daily exercise for professional developers.

In the developer's perfect scenario, they buy low, vary planning permission, develop and sell high. This leads to sites achieving sale sums that seem inflated. They are high for the present-day value but if the improved planning variation is achieved, they are cheap. The danger in this scenario presents itself in two ways. First, if you require finance the lenders surveyor will not attach any premium or increase the valuation on the basis of an expected change of permission. They will strictly value on the current status only. Secondly, if you do not achieve the improved permission, you will have overpaid and will not be able to develop the property as you envisioned.

Opportunities

Subdivision.

The point of this book is for you to owner-build, but occasionally you'll see an opportunity where you can purchase a larger site than you need and subdivide segments of the site into separately titled and separately taxed parcels of land. This allows you to sell off parcels of the site and make a profit. This money can subsidize your site purchase and build costs. Each subdivided parcel will often have a locally determined minimum size. In some zones an existing house can be demolished and two smaller homes constructed on the site.

In this case it would be very helpful to you if the zoned use was planned unit development (PUD).

The local city or town council will want to see evidence that you have taken advantage of land features and natural drainage for surface water. If subdividing, you likely will need to allow for easements for sewers and water supplies and perhaps submit an impact report.

The sting in this tail is that the local town may charge an impact fee *in advance* to cover costs for upgrading local services to meet the new residents' requirements.

Your consultants will prepare a package of information, including plat maps which will detail local data, restrictive covenants, sections, public easements, road access etc. Once the plat map is approved it will be added to the local land records and become the accepted record of your subdivision.

The proposed subdivision must be approved through the land planning process. This is more easily achieved if your proposal meets the current comprehensive or master plan, but you still may need to seek approval through the local zoning board.

Assemblage.

This is the exact opposite of subdivision. It is where you combine adjacent separately titled land parcels into a single larger holding. The idea is that by combining them you are increasing the value of all the land. This increased value is called plottage. This is where you create a new single land parcel for a larger or more expensive house, or if with more surrounding land, a more valuable development.

Enhance Permission.

A different version is where a site has a building permit for a modest home and the site is valued on this basis. Can you enhance the permitted design? If you can lift the site value by improving the currently approved detailed building permit, you can build your enhanced home and enjoy the extra space as well as increase your wealth.

A warning: There are plenty of opportunities to make mistakes when buying a lot. Be careful of lots without a permit to build or those not located in a residential zone. Where a lot is in a residential zone you can be encouraged that a permit will be forthcoming after an appropriate application is lodged. If you can, I strongly recommend that you discuss your proposals with the municipal planning zoning officials to get their take on the likelihood of the issue of a a zoning and/or building permit.

There are benefits to co-operating with a seller. You can sometimes agree to submit a zoning/building permit with the owner's approval. This comes into play where both parties want clarity on the potential of a property. The owner does not want to undersell and the purchaser does not want to pay more than the property is worth. But they both agree a fair amount should be paid.

This 'fair' amount is determined by the response of the planners. If they agree a residential build permit would reasonably be approved, then you have a basis for a valuation. If they find differently, the valuation will be different.

Another way of dealing with this, to eliminate the risk of you purchasing a lot you can't build on, is to offer to purchase subject to the issue of a building permit. In this scenario, you make an offer on the basis of the enhanced permit and, with the owner's approval, an application is submitted. On issue of the permit, you complete the purchase. If a permit is refused, you walk away with your deposit refunded or not, dependent on your agreement. The purchaser is usually liable for all design and permit costs incurred.

Residual Valuation.

If the lot has a building permit, what is its value?

Commonly, a lot has a given market value by the seller or his realtor. This does not mean it is a fair value or what you can afford within your budget. Even if it is considered a fair value inasmuch as the amount others are prepared to pay, only purchase at a price level you can justify.

To assess the value, you can carry out a 'Residual Valuation'. This is a value which leads to an appraisal figure of what the lot is worth on the open market.

Start with the value of the completed project. Once complete, what will the house be worth on the open market? You can research this locally and online and then assess what you can reasonably achieve in a sale by a willing seller to a willing buyer. This means in the normal course of events and not in a rushed or forced sale. This figure is termed the Gross Development Value (GDV).

To determine the value of the lot, you must first compile a list of items needed to owner-build and complete your project and place sums to items on the list as a monetary value. By deducting one value from the other, you can then assess if the project is worthwhile. As a rough guide, the land figure is often found to be approximately between one quarter and one third of the GDV figure. Be cautious with this 'rule of thumb' as the land price as a percentage of cost often exceeds this in high value areas.

Check out the value of other lots and recently completed homes in your area to try and get as close a comparison as you can. It can be worth asking the realtor for a market analysis. You are aware the realtor is paid a commission by the seller but a local comparison may well have been prepared for the seller to have arrived at his sale price offer and all information is useful at this stage. This does not mean that you do not carry out your own research as in the end you are spending your own money.

A further option is to instruct an independent valuation. This will give you a surveyor's opinion and perhaps comfort, although your lender nearly always insists on a further valuation before they will provide finance. They will usually only accept valuations from surveyors already on their approved list, regardless of your valuer's qualifications. You pay for the lender's valuation to prove the value of your purchase to you and to the lender.

The owner-builder has an advantage in this part of the process as they usually want a place to live based on realities: the sum of the cost the lot can be purchased for plus the cost of construction. By contrast, a professional developer must include an additional profit figure.

If the lot does not have a current zoning or building permit for a dwelling, what is its value? First, you must find out what the blocking issues are relative to achieving permission. You can discuss this with the town planners or your designer or urban planning consultant. However, you must establish to your own satisfaction if permission for the potential dwelling will be subject to obstacles such as: conservation area policies, inappropriate zoning, difficulty with covenants, historic preservation requirements etc. Carefully consider the likelihood of achieving a zoning approval and a building permit for the size and type of development you wish to construct.

Some lenders will provide finance for the purchase of lots. Confirm the attitude of your lenders over this point and their view on releasing funds before a zoning and a building permit are in place. Always include your funders within your plans and prepare accordingly.

Site Suitability.

Is your site suitable for the type of house you would like to construct? If the site is on a slope, can you use this to your advantage or would you need to remove large amounts of soil to create a level area? Are your neighbors close by and will there be privacy issues? Will your new structure affect the quality of their light or view? Setback requirements for any building from a boundary or public road must always be considered. You may need to appeal this point as part of the issue of a zoning permit because of on-site conditions, even if the land use zoning permits residential development.

Does the Site Have Good Transport Links?

This can mean access to roads or public transport. The importance of access to public transport is a feature of current debate. Many high density urban authorities would like to reduce street congestion and as a way of doing this, they reject applications with any level of on-site car parking. Some ramp up the pressure by also refusing to issue resident and visitor parking permits for properties created by new developments. Other cities require a minimum number of off-street parking spaces per dwelling. The whole issues of cars as a means of personal transport is becoming politicized and so attitudes can change quickly. Again, check in your location.

Restrictive Conditions & Covenants?

Restrictive Conditions & Covenants (RC&Cs) are rules or restrictions placed on the land that prohibit certain types of development or activity. They are often incorporated in the deed that conveys title to the property. They also 'run with the land', which means they restrict the current owner at that time as well as future owners.

These are created by private parties (previous owners or developers) in order to, for example, maintain access to a certain area or to preserve a 'character' to the land or subdivision. They are also used to prevent certain building uses, densities of development and types or styles of buildings. RC&Cs are often viewed by residents as a protection against others constructing a building that may lessen their own privacy or reduce their property value, or other unwelcome ideas.

An emerging issue particularly relating to infill sites in older urban subdivisions is restrictive covenants that were historically registered against a title. Perhaps, at the time of registration, the restrictions pretty much reflected the zoning in that area but over time, zoning restrictions have changed to meet the needs of growing mixed-use modern urban areas. The covenant is now more onerous than the surrounding zone ordinances in which they are situated. Meanwhile the city/town/municipal authorities are only concerned that developments meet the current zoning requirements. Therefore, it is conceivable that a proposed development can meet the municipal zoning but not the restrictive covenant. It can mean that to overturn the restriction, you'd need to get written permission from all affected parties (neighbors included) or else a court has to be satisfied that the restrictive covenant is no longer reasonable or relevant and it can be lifted.

In subdivided residential areas RC&Cs are overseen by the Homeowners Association (HOA) who are empowered to enforce RC&Cs. The HOA, are set up by the developer who wishes to provide comfort for purchasers. When a certain percentage of properties are sold the residents take charge and form a management body. Many RC&Cs are time limited from a set enactment date, typically either 10 or 25 years. After this, they become inoperative unless the HOA, through a representative vote, extends the period or changes the RC&Cs.

The purpose of Deed Restrictions and RC&Cs is to protect property value or address occupational health and safety concerns as well as to put reasonable constraints on residents' development or change of properties within the estate. These can be determined as invalid if they prevent the free transfer of property and they must not promote any illegal activity such as excluding certain races or ethnic/religious groups. It may well be the case that private land use controls may be more limiting to the houseowner than public zoning as it may well deal with micro matters over the size of garden sheds, fence materials or prohibiting a visible satellite dish.

Only by checking leases and deeds will you find out if any deed restrictions or covenants exist that are detrimental to your plans. Realtors will often list property for sale and perhaps not fully cover this aspect in their description as you would like. If you find your lot has old covenants that can be technically called on, even if this is unlikely, you may have to reassure yourself and your lender. This may be achieved by the seller taking out a special insurance to cover all such eventualities.

Public Footpaths.

Are there any footpaths adjacent to your land or over your land? Footpaths can appear unused but they still might be relied upon by members of the public. Any such indications of public access must be considered in order to see how it affects your use of the lot. The Plat map should indicate any covenants or rights.

No owner-builder wants unexpected costs or obligations. By taking out a simple single-payment insurance policy, most of these costs can be insured against. Consider approaching the seller to pay for this insurance and include the benefit of this within the sale terms.

Other covenants – such as conditions binding you to, say, only construct a boundary wall with a particular material or to protect views from neighbouring properties – can all be considered and the agreed sale price amended to reflect these conditions

Easements (Covenants in Reverse).

The opposite to a covenant can also be an issue and it's called an easement. For example, the seller assures you they have used a driveway or access for decades, but in reality, they do not have explicit consent to do so. Equally, you may notice that a neighbor crosses the property regularly for a specific purpose. Perhaps other property owners have also used this access without explicit permission. This is where permitted use has created a 'right of way'. Again, you can ask the seller to take out insurance, underwriting your costs, protecting you if this access becomes a point of dispute in the future.

The interesting thing about these insurances is they are rarely called upon. But if they were called upon, will the insurer play ball? Lenders and conveyancers seem to find them comforting.

> **TIP BOX**
>
> The legal definitions are:
>
> Absolute Covenants – prohibit something completely.
>
> Qualified Covenants – a third party's consent is required.
>
> Fully Qualified Covenants – a third party's consent must not be unreasonably withheld.
>
> Easement Appurtenant – this allows the owner of a property the use of a neighbour's land.
>
> Dominant Tenement – the land that benefits from the use.
>
> Servient Tenement – the land that is used.
>
> *In plain language, an easement over land transfers to the new owner.* Property owners can petition the court to remove covenants under certain circumstances.

Easement by Agreement.

An easement can be created by agreement of two parties in writing or it is recorded in the deed of conveyance. This clearly states what the conditions of the easement are and that it will 'run with the property' and so be transferred to subsequent owners.

Easement by Necessity.

An easement is created by a landowner selling a parcel of land which can only be accessed by crossing the vendor's remaining land. Courts have upheld the principle that owners have a right to access and exit their land. The term *necessity* is key. If another less convenient way of accessing the land is available without crossing over the seller's land then this easement may not be available.

Easement by Prescription.

If a person has continuously crossed over land for an extended period (generally 10 to 21 years) in the owner's knowledge but without explicit permission then an easement by prescription may have been acquired. Interestingly, by succession, a new owner can continue a use on from a previous owner or an inheritor by tacking (combining) their periods of use.

The purposes of this book do not include giving legal advice. Many special circumstances apply that are unanswered, for example:

- Under what circumstances can you terminate an easement?
- What if the term-of-use has not reached your province or state's minimum length of time?
- Is a license the same as an easement?
- What is adverse possession?
- Can insurance be taken out to cover a perceived risk?
- Are cartways or driveways necessary, reasonable and just?

These are all good questions as are many more that should only be covered by engaging a lawyer and listening to what is said. Property owners can petition the court to remove covenants under certain circumstances but as with all matters legal, take advice from a lawyer and then get a second opinion.

Realtors.

Realtors have duties of disclosure and are bound by codes of ethics but they will often do what they can to protect themselves from possible charges of liability over misrepresentation. In this litigious world they would be remiss not to seek protection from any accusations that they knew certain information important to the purchaser but did not disclose it. I am not charging that realtors will withhold information or mislead the purchaser, but I am saying that as the purchaser, you must not fully rely on their statements. Neither should you take comfort in the security of pursuing them for recompense later if you feel you were not as informed as you should have been.

Overage.

Overage or *claw back provisions* are to be carefully thought through, with the benefit of legal advice. These are provisions added to an agreement in the case of something occurring at a future time.

An example could be the sale of a large detached house on a substantial lot. The seller seeks to benefit from a future increase in the value of the lot by the new owner achieving an enhanced planning permission. Here, the seller would retain a covenant that he will only relax by the payment of a sum which reflects an uplift in value. In simple terms, you pay them a further sum of money as you have increased the value of the land through an improved building permit. These agreements are often for a fixed number of years. Indeed, agreements without an end date can be problematic.

Gazumping.

Another one to watch is gazumping of your intended purchase. Until you have signed the contract to purchase the land, there is a risk of another purchaser stepping in and gazumping - or purchasing ahead of you. Realtors and lawyers are supposed to discourage this behavior but in the end, they must accept instructions from their clients and nothing is agreed until the contract is signed. If more than one interested party makes an offer, the realtor may look for best and final bids as a way of determining the highest offer. After the offer is made by the purchaser and deposit accepted by the seller you are in a contract - not before that point.

Taking an Option.

If another purchaser stepping in and having their offer accepted is a concern and you are absolutely sure you want to purchase, you can ask the seller for a *'lock out agreement'* or *'option agreement'*. This binds the seller to sell only to you for an agreed fixed period. If this approach is taken, it is normal for you both to agree a contract which secures the lot, but as optionor you will pay a non-refundable sum. This sum is not in addition to the purchase price but rather a first stage payment. When a purchaser decides not to proceed after having entered an option agreement, they usually believe it is for a good reason. Frequently they feel that something has turned up that stops them from proceeding while the seller believes that they are suffering from a case of buyer's remorse. This usually begins a serious discussion on the return of the non-refundable deposit. Experienced lawyers are often reluctant in advising their respective clients to get involved in option agreements to stop this situation before it starts.

The seller may also link the option to an overage agreement, with the price he receives, dependent on your success in receiving approval for an enhanced permit.

In option agreements, however, the key is the term 'non-refundable'. If you are unclear on what this means, you definitely need professional legal advice before proceeding.

TRUE STORY

A lower court case dealing with boundary dimensions, and Court of Appeal overturning the initial finding, was played out in 2019 in Ontario. The case centred around the seller of a lot not providing accurate dimensions of the length of the boundaries and the purchaser not checking, even though the sales details advised "depths to be verified". Accurate dimensions could have been gleaned from the deed, an online land survey, the plan of subdivision or even by instructing the only person qualified to measure in Ontario, a land surveyor to confirm the boundary length.

They did none of these things and a legal battle ensued over a $100K deposit plus lawyer's fees and court costs. Always ensure the lot's boundary configuration, dimensions and size are clear.

Will Trees be Removed?

If you seek to remove any trees as part of your proposal, check if a Tree Ordinance is in place in your community. Several states and provinces encourage their cities and towns to adopt an ordinance but it is far from universal. Will all trees to be removed need to be specifically included on your building permit application? For example, the Seattle Municipal Code (SMC) requires a Tree & Vegetation

Removal Permit in certain conditions. SMC recognizes individual trees and groups of trees designated as 'Exceptional Trees' and are listed for protection. The City of Vancouver, Canada has similar 'Protection of Tree By-laws' that explicitly state the procedures and what evidence you must provide to receive a tree removal permit.

A Tree Ordinance may require you to produce an arborist's report and mark up trees scheduled for removal while protecting those remaining. Will you need to replace trees to compensate for those removed? Will your neighbors' trees affect levels of daylight within your proposed home? Raise these points with your consultants.

Are Services Connected (Water, Gas, Electricity, Sewers etc.)?

It is important you visually inspect the lot and confirm the location of all services. The services that are already connected and where they are situated may or may not be listed in the sale details, so check there first. The site plat map may be useful in locating services and easements.

If any of the services you will require are not connected, contact the services supplier and check availability. This is especially important in rural areas, where not all services are available. Find out a ballpark figure for getting missing services connected and include a suitable sum in the budget.

Finance.

Finance costs must be included in your spreadsheet. These are all costs resulting from the development. If you need to sell another property to fund this project, then all selling costs must be included, along with any bridging finance costs payable.

Include all costs up to the point of completion and the start of the long-term mortgage on your home. Remember, legal fees and stamp duties/transfer taxes must be paid and accounted for. British Columbia has brought in a broad-based carbon tax and some states and local areas may bring in an environmental tax, one that goes by the name of something like 'infrastructure levy' or 'carbon contribution'. This does vary across cities, counties and towns. Some areas charge the seller not the buyer so as with all other legal/planning matters find out about your local situation and if a tax is due, find out when it is paid.

Are There Any Pollutants?

There may be pollutants under the ground from a previous site use. This can be a concern when you are building on Brownfield/Greenfield sites, which are sites that have had a previous industrial, commercial or agricultural use. Lots that have previously been used for residential purposes are not covered by the Brownfield Law, so be careful. For example, check if an existing fuel tank was ever buried (fully or partially) as leakage over years can cause pollution.

Your neighbors might have seasonal odours arising from certain occupations, such as farming, or the lot may be under the flight paths of nearby airports. If in the vicinity of an airport, your land may be subject to a requirement that you soundproof your house from their noise.

One point to consider, which will not be apparent on a visual inspection, is the likelihood of Radon gas on your site. Radon is a gas found in North America. Radon is a colorless, inert radioactive gas that can be dangerous to health in confined spaces whilst harmless in open spaces. If you need to protect against this gas, membranes can be installed as part of the floor makeup, which act as a barrier. You can check the probability of a Radon-affected lot online or with your local environmental agency.

If you are concerned, raise the issues with your designer and engineer.

Ecology and Biodiversity.

State and province authorities give a high level of protection to wildlife and their habitats. Identification of the site environment may have to be carried out early in the planning process to help balance the relationship between plants, wildlife and people.

Site clearance of trees and plants/undergrowth will greatly impact the environment and you may be expected to offer a solution. Local planning guidance is often looking for damage limitation and mitigation. Therefore, plan site clearance or demolition work carefully and avoid nesting, hibernation and breeding seasons. Ensure protective fences are in place and are effective. Watercourses must be kept clean and pollutant free. Confirm compliance by producing method statements and work in line with local environmental management plans. Native animal habitat and native planting can be a sensitive subject. The Environmental Protection Agency (EPA) in the US and North American Waterfowl Management Plan in

Canada promote the retention of wetland areas and clean waterways. It is crucial you are aware of any and all obligations should your land be in the vicinity of a natural wetlands.

Is the Area Changing?

Are you aware of any infrastructure changes to the area? What other developments are in the pipeline? Change can be positive or negative. Be aware of any proposals for your area and assess how they can affect your new home.

Public Auctions.

Auctions tie in the seller and buyer from the moment of the 'fall of the hammer'. If you buy at auction, it is an irrevocable agreement. You must be sure of the maximum figure you can pay, regardless of the price others offer, and you must be confident you have fully assessed the lot. The same points apply to online auctions which are currently increasing in popularity.

Be aware what costs are included in public auctions. The auction pack will state (perhaps in legalese) what charges are to be paid to the auctioneer as commission *on top of your bid*. It is not unknown for buyers to include fees or payment of their side's legal fees, particularly on lower value lots. If you ask the question, you should be told what fees and costs will be added to the winning offer. Buyer beware!

Decision Time

The site assessment is crucial. You need to focus on whether you will move ahead with your proposal at this location or not. You have to make a decision on a whole range of issues outside of the merits of site suitability. By methodically following this process, you can come to a considered view. Property purchase is never an easy choice to make and there are always issues you can further consider. In the end you must make the call.

Chapter 2 – Action

- Investigate possibilities through the 'six degrees of separation'
- Instruct a lawyer
- Meet with your designer on site to discuss
- Discuss CC&Rs and zoning
- Do not proceed to a legally binding contract unless you are absolutely sure of what you are doing

WHICH TECHNOLOGIES?
Solar
GSHP
MMC

ASSESS PLOT
Discuss Site With Designer
Site Visit
Site Assessment
Planner Discussion

TEAM
Set Up Files
Talk to Financial Advisor
Family Support
Magazine Articles
Set Up Basic Accounts
Legal Advice

MONEY
Get Offer For Finance
Make Offer

CHAPTER 3
SUMMARY

The program sets the whole tone for your design. But, how do you know what you want?

Interesting things covered by this chapter include:

- Discuss with your family what you are trying to achieve
- Determine how long the whole process will take
- How can the design be exceptional?
- What can you do to futureproof?

CHAPTER 3

DEFINE YOUR REQUIREMENTS

'What we call the beginning is often the end. And to make an end is to make a beginning. The end is where we start from'.
— T. S. Eliot

In the 'beginning', you should address a few fundamental points.

What Are You Trying To Do?

It may seem obvious: you want to build a new home, however, the question of what specific outcomes you are trying to achieve should be addressed.

Do you want to create a special house on a specific lot… or do you want to create something similar to other houses available but at a cheaper cost? Consider who will live in this house… what are their needs in relation to living areas and numbers of bedrooms? Is it a full-time home or a holiday retreat?

Can You Dream Before You Have Purchased a Lot?

Yes, you can dream and scheme, although without a lot you will not be taken seriously by professionals. In fact, dreaming and scheming can be valuable. If you have realistically looked at your position overall, if you have looked at your family and their needs and pieced together a rough plan, then when you actively look at lots, you'll have an idea of what your requirements are.

Are you wishing to owner-build to achieve a different home to those available to purchase in your selected area? Do you want more house for less money or are you more concerned with ecological issues and trying to reduce or eliminate the carbon footprint of your home?

There can be any number of reasons for going on this journey, and it's important you express what your reasons are. Your reasons should be considered as a number of joined up points making a whole, rather than as isolated points.

I find *if I cannot write it down – I cannot do it*. Meaning, after writing down what you intend to do in detail, flaws in the logic may become obvious. Only after these issues are addressed satisfactorily should you proceed.

These written points are also useful in other ways. When it's time to explain the benefits of owner-building to your family or to a lender, you will have considered the whole process and are able to articulate the pros and cons of the project. You can show you fully understand what it is you are taking on.

What Form will the Design Take?

Moving on from Jigsaw, you should discuss your aspirations for the house with your designer. This will dictate the whole direction of the build and what type of home you want to build. This is a fun part of the process as you can imagine different elements of design and what your dream inclusions are.

Have you seen a house or style you admire and would like to follow or are you bound by external elevations, which are driven by the locality and adjoining properties? What design boundaries can you push? For example, can you cleverly conceal your home in the landscape or design a modern eco home within a traditional outer skin?

How Long Should the Whole Process Take?

Obviously, this depends on what you are building, but you need to be aware of the timings of the pre-construction phase as well as the construction and post construction phases. The clearer you become on the actual design and selection of materials, the clearer the designs become, to the point where they are fixed. Once they are fixed, you can get fixed prices and uncertainty lessens. This is the start of the balance between Cost, Quality, Safety and Speed of construction.

Pre-Construction Phase

Getting Organized.

The clock starts when you have located the land and agreed a contract to purchase. The traditional process from offer to purchase and completion of the sale is 4 to 6 weeks. At Auction the usual period from sale until completion of the purchase is 28 days. Obviously, funds are needed to complete the purchase to these or the agreed timescales.

During this time, you can make a start on the planning application or amendments and put your team of consultants on notice of the deadlines. You will also need to produce your business plan and meet and agree finance with your lender. Through discussions with the designer and engineer, you should specifically agree the build method and decide which work you will carry out and which will be undertaken by contractors.

The designer will in the first instance prepare a design for submission to the local planning department. Often input is required from a structural engineer and your designer should discuss this with you. Planning departments publish timescales and commitments on their websites for their application processing times and this is a good place to start your assessment.

Program.

The program (or brief) is perhaps the most important document in any part of the owner-build journey. It sets out clearly what it is you want and leads you to how best to achieve it.

The more guidance you can give in this process, the more the designer will get an accurate idea of your needs. I am not saying you have prepared and finalised the brief for the designer but rather, you have already considered your needs and are able to effectively communicate them.

Communication is the First and Most Important Point.

The program is a process which leads the designer in the direction the client wants to go. So, rather than advising you on what they consider you need, the designer will listen to your views and try to produce a scheme which meets your requirements.

Designers start their project discussions with a client and write up a program only once a lot has been secured. They are invariably reluctant to discuss design without an actual lot. Many designers will, within reason, advise you on the suitability of a lot if you find one you are keen on. It certainly can be useful to have a detached and independent professional view on the potential of the lot. They will help you focus on issues affecting site suitability. A good local house designer should be able to look out for natural features of the site and tell you if any items of planning must be considered before you commit to purchase.

> **TRUE STORY**
>
> I was driving across town for a site visit one day, with the project architect as a passenger. We were discussing external fencing and took a small diversion to look at a fence on a one-year old house I had noticed while under construction. The fence had interesting features and with a little tweaking a revamped design would be perfect for the new home we were constructing. The house owner came out and asked why we were taking photos of his home. We explained that we admired the home, especially the fence and the owner was very pleased to accept our praise and happy to discuss their build experiences in detail. He passed on a few hard won tips on constructing the fence, which were useful. If you admire a property, do not be afraid to mention this to the owners. Who knows, you may even learn something.

How Do You Analyze What it is You Want?

First, describe what it is you want in writing. This can be by list in The 1-Page Owner-Builder Plan or written out in full. What facilities do you want to provide for your family? Even obvious facilities should be listed. Kitchen, living areas, bedrooms, how many rooms or zones, the garage, and what should be next to each other. If you have purchased a lot, are there, for example, restrictions on the allowed heights of the building? Or is it located in a conservation area?

You can assist this process by visiting exhibitions and reading magazines and real estate lift-outs. Take a look at how others have tackled space and layouts. This is the point you can start to personalize your home, not later on when the floor plans have been set.

When you have a list of potential rooms and areas, all of which have obvious uses, it's interesting to consider what else these spaces are used for. What kind of spaces would you like? Are they large and open plan, leading from one family area to another, or do you want a mix of open and private?

At this stage, it's important you are realistic on potential uses. When you have completed your use schedule, you may well find that the space required to meet all the design wish-list points becomes unmanageably large. The Program Schedule is a notional schedule of spaces and your requirements. It is not a full list and is a little tongue-in-cheek. When completing your list, it should be personalized to you and your family. This is a valuable exercise because for the first time you are stating in writing what it is you want from your home. By writing it down and discussing this list with your home team, it makes the whole project real and not just a distant dream.

What Do You Learn?

You may find that the areas on your wish list, when brought together, will indicate a very large home which will probably exceed your budget and have horrendously expensive running costs. Let's temper this. Can spaces be used for multiple purposes? And will the home as initially designed deal effectively with a growing and changing family unit?

What Do You Get Out of Owner-Building Your Own Home?

Let's get an idea of the home building landscape. Cost apart, people moving home across the country do not have great difficulty in replacing their old house with a very similar home in another region. Many home builders have repeated what works and with good cause. It's efficient to give both the building authorities and the people what they want.

The building authorities like to approve homes in the center of the norm as they tend to comply with codes and standards. They conform and are energy efficient, with minimum sizes of rooms and so on. The individual officer may like something a little more special but the system does not critique the boring and nondescript.

The volume builders find it efficient to build to set plans and standards and thus do not have to produce individual answers relying on *standard detailing*. These standard designs are repeated over many sites and as such, guarantees that the buildings as designed comply at the most basic level.

This approach generally taken by the North American construction industry has been criticized by Ombudsmen's reports in Canada. Indeed, a search of the web soon finds pages of complaints on problems with large-volume builders in the US. They found:

- Problems recording the work carried out and audit trails for decisions and installations.
- Ignorance of regulations and guidance of those who need it most.
- Indifference to quality, to produce quickly and cheaply while using ambiguity of regulations to game the system.
- Lack of clarity on roles and responsibilities.
- Inadequate regulatory oversight.

A recent class action pursued by residents of a Texas development over poor construction quality of their homes alleged that the builder had only offered a list of "vague and non-committal repairs" that would have used "cheap cosmetic fixes". Whatever the truth of any individual development it appears that some homes offered for sale as having a high quality structure and finish may not be all that they seem.

There are good builders everywhere but large companies do follow *group think* and often the immediate shareholder profits can be the guiding light for private companies.

That all said, your vision can be totally different. By taking command of your own home build, you can choose who you work with and the quality of the home you build. Realtors often list a home for sale as a 'builder's own home' or 'ex-show home', which refers to the belief that to build for yourself or build under scrutiny will result in a higher quality of finish than may otherwise be achieved.

TRUE STORY

IT and smart home features are becoming the norm and yes, allowing space for hobbies and interests can be desirable. However, I have seen lots of custom-built homes which include desirable but underused custom-built features.

The fashion for Billiard Rooms to give the 'boys' somewhere to congregate seems to have faded, I suspect; more pool tables are underused than overused. I was recently at a new home and was proudly given the grand tour. The

> layout was personalised and the owners had carefully considered the kitchen and laundry room spaces and seemed to work well. They had built in a fully air conditioned home cinema room with stepped floors and cinema style seating. I asked how they were enjoying the room and they admitted that the 'cutting edge' visual equipment was now old technology and was no longer marketed or technically supported. The layout of the room, with bolted down seats on a stepped platform, restricted other uses and so it was not functioning anymore. Each to their own, but to save space and not waste money, try to live the dream as opposed to just dreaming of the dream. Flexible spaces are much more useful!

Futureproof.

The home should be adaptable, so as family circumstances change, you can change your home layout. Flexibility of spaces and designs means you can, through forward planning, amend or introduce new features without major disruptions.

An example of this would be you planning at some future point to extend the home by building an extension. How much future-proofing should you incorporate? You could extend the foundations underneath the rear yard surface, have a drain connection available, run sealed power cables ready for future connections or even have a section of wall built in a way that it can be removed without major work. By foreseeing probable needs, you can reduce future work and disruption.

This all feeds into the concept of 'Lifetime' homes, which means designing the house so it is suitable for you and your partner to remain in occupation throughout the different (and natural) phases of life. What is required as reasonable access for a fit 40-year old can be markedly different for a stiff 60-year old.

Savings.

Money-saving can also be a motivation. You can either get a better house for less money than a finished house would cost or you can gain value by doing it yourself, saving the cost of hiring someone else. If this independence is linked to a desire to achieve a high-quality finish with the satisfaction of creating something special yourself, well so much the better. This also allows you to build your home in sections and complete as the funds are available.

The possible flaw in the argument can be your eventual mortgage. This mortgage will be dependent on the house being complete and signed off as habitable. This means completion speed is of the essence, as you will wish to transition from a more expensive development mortgage to a cheaper residential mortgage.

Skillset.

What are your skill sets and how do you feel about expanding your skills, often outside your comfort zone? Take a serious look at your own experience and set out what duties you are prepared to pass onto to others and what physical roles you'll undertake.

Another skill is reading drawings and specifications, and understanding (gleaning as often as not) what the document is trying to advise you on. This can be difficult but as with everything, practice makes… 'better'. Financial understanding and budgeting are also crucial and a firm grip is needed on this.

Finally, you need to be a self-starter, with bags of motivation and energy. Anything less will be a trial of endurance and an outcome with no guaranteed winner!

Pattern Language Vs. The List.

We all come at things from a different viewpoint. One way to design and build was promoted by Christopher Alexander in ***A Pattern Language: Towns, Buildings, Construction,*** and an opposite approach taken by Ken Sherott in ***Your House and How to Build It.***

Is Anyone Right and Anyone Wrong?

Ken Sherrott was writing in the post-WW2 era of practicality and getting on with things whereas Christopher Alexander was writing in the post-hippie world of the 1970s. Even so, over this time, the basic and practical points of designing and building your own home hardly changed and they are still relevant today. We do, in this modern time, place emphasis on insulation, green materials and smart homes. The increase in regulation since an earlier and simpler time is also astounding, but the basics stay the same.

The more fluid of the two, Alexander starts with descriptive terms for what it is your heart desires and how you explain to your designer what you want.

'Consider the site and its buildings as a single living ecosystem. Leave those areas that are most precious, beautiful, comfortable, and healthy as they are, and build new structures in those parts of the site which are least pleasant now'.

Alexander also introduces the concept of an Intimacy Gradient:

'Unless the spaces in a building are arranged in a sequence which corresponds to their degree of privateness, the visits made by strangers, friends, guests, clients, family, will always be a little awkward'.

Alexander recognizes 253 different patterns, all of which set the tone of how he encourages you to approach the design of your living and sleeping zones in a spiritual and philosophical manner.

Ken Sherrott would not have recognized this style and process. He was list driven. He does not merely recommend but goes further and categorically states the 25 factors you should make a fixed and firm decision on. With matters decided, you are off and running. For him, these decisions are not only taken before the design is formulated, the design becomes a reflection of his list.

The list includes:

- Total floor area
- Number of bedrooms
- Separate living and dining areas
- Separate entrance hallway
- Laundry
- Built-in-wardrobes in all bedrooms
- WC/ toilet accessible from the common areas and the rear porch
- How the house is positioned on the lot
- Landscaping of the garden

This list goes on, with ever-increasing degrees of specific instruction.

Alexander tends to speak in abstract concepts, while Sherrott is concerned Dad will not have a long distance to travel between rear yard and toilet! It's worth taking a wider view of very different design ideas before deciding 'your way'.

The journey is essential, for without the journey, how can you make decisions? The program is fundamental but on this journey *the destination* is what's important.

The designer wants to know what your views are and how he or she can best help you crystalize your vision.

Chapter 3 – Action

Visit trade shows and read builder, home design and interior style magazines

- Help your designer to come up with something special
- Try to fix on a house 'style'

MONEY
Access Funds
Identify Future Leverage
Prepare Comprehensive Document For Lender

DESIGN
Brief
Discuss Structure
Technologies & Smart Home Technology
Magazine Articles
Come Up With Something 'Special'

LEGAL
Liaise with Lawyer
Caveat Emptor
Know Your Client

CHAPTER 4
SUMMARY

Caveat Emptor – Buyer Beware is the most important concept in this chapter.

Highlights covered in this chapter include:

- A number of things could go wrong but these can be eliminated by a good team around you
- Prepare for completion/settlement by having your finance in order
- Points to check before agreement to purchase
- Closing
- After completion of the purchase

CHAPTER 4

THE LEGAL BIT

'More Law, Less Justice'.
— Marcus Tullius Cicero

Conveyancing is a legal term for buying or selling property. Lawyers traditionally carried out this work, although in some provinces in Canada Notary Publics prepare the sales documentation for both seller and buyer.

Your conveyancer will advise you over basic general restrictions that legally relate to the purchase. This will cover any leases or listed and registered conditions found on the title. It is outside of their expertise to advise on planning matters not part of the registered title and attached conditions.

Having a lawyer or conveyancer is a 'necessity' in contractual situations where you are selling or purchasing property. If the sale is in any way complex or legal proceedings are even mentioned in passing during the construction process, get a lawyer. In order for lawyers to give maximum benefit to their clients, they specialize their practice in certain areas of expertise. As most work in small, local offices, these specialists should be easy enough to find.

When you are purchasing land or selling property, you should instruct a lawyer who is comfortable with conveyancing and the property law as it applies to all parties.

Lawyers come into their own in times of trouble. If you start to slide into a dispute with a contractor or supplier, with the possibility of issuing legal proceedings, you need someone comfortable with litigation within the construction industry. You can run these issues past your designer or cost engineer, who can both give industry-specific guidance, but as matters progress, specialist lawyers become involved.

The mark of a good lawyer is someone who finds ways of achieving a satisfactory result without resorting to direct legal action and all the related cost and uncertainty this brings. However, if a problem progresses to litigation, you need a legal partner you can rely on. There are always legal procedures to be followed and difficult forms to complete, and with your lawyer's advice they can then be filled in correctly.

Your relationship with your lawyers must be positive and open. They can only offer frank and sage advice if they are aware of all the facts. Your lawyer should explain the law to you by breaking it down and clarifying how it applies to you. This is to assist you to meet your obligations and comply by taking the appropriate action.

The legal aspect of the owner-build can be crucial if you are purchasing a lot for your build. A lawyer should always represent you in the purchase process. Where possible, the lawyer should advise you before you verbally make an offer to purchase, or if not, certainly before you legally commit to purchase. There are many legal misconceptions around house/land purchasing and sales. You need straightforward, unadulterated advice not to fall into the many traps set for the unwary.

As with any other professional you employ, you must feel confident in their abilities and expertise. Lawyers will provide indicative quotations for property conveyancing, since the days of 'dusty' lawyer's offices, billing at discretion and not interacting with clients is long past. Have a look at how the quotation is put together. Is it a lump sum or based on an hourly rate, with different partners, lawyers and support staff charged at different rates? Then see if disbursements such as photocopying, telephone calls, etc. are included or will be recorded and individually charged.

Lawyers in Canada and the US have to be licenced in the state or province where you are purchasing the property. If you live in a different state/province you may well need to employ a lawyer in your home state/province and in the area of your purchase. Check your particular situation.

If you are selling a property as well as purchasing, I advise that you keep both transactions separate but with the same lawyer. Seek individual quotations and instruct both matters separately. This approach allows the lawyer to understand the big picture of obligations to existing lenders and match them up with your obligations to new lenders. It may well be that you have to repay a lender to meet the obligations of a mortgage on an existing property at completion but also receive funds on completion for a new mortgage from a new lender.

Real estate agents or realtors sometimes provide 'binders' that they encourage you to sign that resemble legal contracts to purchase. They are not legally binding and are discouraged as they create confusion. Only rely on a lawyer-to-lawyer contract that once signed by both parties is legally acceptable and only sign this after advice from your lawyer.

Occasionally, land developers try to encourage sales by offering to cover fees or taxes for the purchasers. It can be unwise to accept an offer of 'Free Legals' because you normally have to instruct their in-house or preferred legal team to benefit from this offer. Regardless of their assurances of separation of advisors, you cannot be sure you would receive independent advice you can rely on. I always feel it is inappropriate for the seller to choose the purchaser's advisers and so you should instruct an independent lawyer.

Canada and the US have introduced legislation regarding the mortgage finance industry and these cover many issues to protect the consumer. The US has the Truth in Lending Act (TILA) and Real Estates Settlement Procedures Act (RESPA) and Canada has their Canada Mortgage and Housing Corporation (CMHC). You do not need to become expert in the acts but realize that the market is regulated and highly controlled.

On the point of a developer covering your tax obligations or indeed any other inducement, it is important to make all the purchase details clear to your lawyer and your mortgage provider. The lawyer will advise you on what purchase figure you need to state on the land registry or other legal documents, while your lender needs to know the specific cost details of your purchase.

To do otherwise can lead to you reporting incorrect figures, which can have serious consequences for you. If lenders feel they were misled they can withdraw offers of finance and governments take possible underpayment of tax seriously.

Different legal systems exist across different states and countries but certain basic principles are adopted across western style administrations. Law is divided into two types: Civil and Criminal law. We are only concerned with civil law in a property purchase. Your lawyer will advise you through the following stages and will alert you to potential pitfalls.

Before Purchase Agreement

All sales agreements must start with an offer and an acceptance. The seller offers to sell at a certain price and the buyer agrees to purchase. From this point, you are at the highest risk as far as wasted fees are concerned. You offered to purchase the lot, and if accepted, the seller's lawyer collates and supplies the following documents :

- The title deeds
- Survey
- Title Insurance policy
- Existing mortgages or promissory notes attached to the property
- Certificates of Occupancy (if applicable)
- Tax bills
- Utility and fuel bills - if existing lot has a property
- Any leases or associated documents

Your lawyer will review the financial conditions of the purchase as well as all the documents produced. They will try to 'look behind them' so that they can fully advise you on any legal matter and warn you of any issues or dangers.

Searches.

Searches on property are both formal and informal. Informally talk to neighbors and people around the area, who often say surprising things. The local collective memory can be a wonderful thing and real 'secrets' can be disclosed. Formally, your lawyer advises you on searches before you purchase.

The searches include the following:

Easements – These can work both *for* the owner and *against* the owner. The easement may allow right to lights or waterways or rights of way. Equally, they can allow others, rights of way and so on.

Restrictive covenants – This is a burden to stop something happening. Possibly you cannot build on the lot or alter a building without the consent of a third party. Perhaps no pets or certain animals are allowed, or even in an ex-church, no alcohol! You potentially take on the breaches of the seller as the 'rights run with the land' and you become the responsible owner.

Planning history – What permit applications have been made and how many were unsuccessful? How were permit applications dealt with by the planners and were any objections received? Does the lot have any current build permits issued and will they work for you?

Local town searches – This will cover ownership of roads affecting the property. Are the local authorities aware of compulsory purchasing of property in the suburb for major infrastructure work, such as roads, airports, etc? Are you able to remove trees or are they protected by a tree ordinance? Are any road widening schemes proposed?

You will be interested in information about existing water connections and sewers. Are a neighbor's sewers running through your property? Water authority information can be private or semi-public, so can be different to information provided by the local town clerks office. Always visually check for signs of underground drainage as records can be incomplete or wrong. A plat map should be included as part of the information package and this can be a very informative document.

Company search – If the seller is a company, are they properly constituted and legally able to sell the property?

Does state-owned or 'buffer' zoned land adjoin the property? – This could potentially raise issues when seeking a build permit further along the journey. Some municipalities seek to camouflage or ease the borders of different zones and may be more concerned with height or visual appearance at these points.

Lender searches – If you are purchasing with the aid of a lender, then your lawyer will often act for you and them. They will usually require evidence you are not subject to bankruptcy proceedings. If you have a common name you may also have to confirm you are not the person who shares your name and their financial difficulties were not yours!

Nightmares.

The following nightmares do happen… but need not happen to you. After purchase, the new buyer finds:

- The land cannot be built on
- The land has a legal impediment stopping them developing it as desired
- They do not have sole unencumbered title to the land
- The land cannot have a house that meets their requirements built on it

I'm sure you'd agree, the likelihood of these nightmares occurring must be managed and minimized. The first three points can be avoided by careful investigation before signing contracts to purchase. Therefore, your lawyer and architect/planning consultant must be given a chance to look at your lot and specifically advise you.

The Land Cannot Be Built On.

This can only be the case if the land is not zoned or suitable for residential development. Not only is this the case, there is also no reasonable expectation you are able to achieve this permit. This problem is one for your planning consultant and the municipality. There are many reasons land is not considered suitable for development: zoning, conservation areas, back land developments and a whole host of regulations. Sometimes the reasons puzzle you and sometimes the reasons are understandable but it matters not, as the result is: the new buyer owns land they cannot build on.

The Land Has a Legal Impediment Stopping the Buyer's Ideal Development.

This is a big reason to consult your lawyer. They will examine the deeds and advise over issues of title or if any outside parties have easements or any rights.

Perhaps covenants or conditions are in place that will restrict design choices or materials to be used or heights of buildings. On some land, underground services cannot be built over, thus not allowing development.

The New Buyer Does Not Have Sole Unencumbered Title to the Land.

Title is key, and what you are looking for is *unencumbered title*. Your lawyer will review the deeds and check you are purchasing the plot without restriction and you have full title. Issues can arise if original deeds have been lost or are simply not available. They will check if there are registered rights of way by foot or vehicle - you will need to visually determine if 'accepted' footpaths crossover any part of the land?

The Land Cannot Have a House to Meet the Buyer's Requirements Built on It.

This last one is the most difficult issue to spot before the sale completes. The lot title search may report back as suitable for development and the title is unencumbered. This is not enough; it has to be suitable for you and your specific development. Do you have to comply with local covenants over the size of your building? Your lawyer cannot be expected to be aware of the size of house you may intend to construct at a later time. Discuss any such restrictions with your designer.

What can Possibly Go Wrong to Stop You Developing?

Just about anything!

- Are the boundaries indicated correctly?
- Does the lot have a noxious weed, which will need to be expensively tackled?
- Will issues of right-of-light-and-air to neighboring properties arise?
- Do you have services or can you get them?
- Does the site cover a main sewer or feature which cannot be built over? Be aware that sewers are not always noted as easements and so other enquiries should be made.
- Check with your legal team/planning consultant that it's reasonable to expect to be able to develop the lot.
- Can you get permission to build a house which suits your needs?
- If the lot already has a build permit, check all the easements are OK with your lawyer.
- Find out if you can personalize the scheme that's stated on the permission.

Compliant Permit.

Sometimes sellers get a build permit but they *never intend to build*. They get what is termed a 'compliant' permission, which meets the planner's requirements and so is easier to achieve. They have then increased the value for sale purposes. Can you personalize the design to meet your needs?

Surely, you may well think, all the above points will come up in the searches. Yes, they should, but each year lot owners are left holding the site when the music stops. If your advisors are reluctant or not positive, do not move to the next stage until you fully understand the risks and are prepared to accept them.

If your lawyer raises negative points, you have three options:

- Carry on regardless
- Seek changes to the sale or reduce your offer
- Withdraw your offer to purchase

Once your lawyer informs you of all the risks involved, you will take the decision. If you withdraw, you may be liable to meet your lawyer's expenses without any hope of contribution from the seller. This is all at your risk. It sounds bad, but I never worry about this cost as I feel the lawyer has protected you from greater loss down the line.

TRUE STORY

My lawyer raised an unusual query on the deeds of a property. The property had not been subject to sale in over 100 years and a charge from before 1920 was listed on the deeds. The person who raised the charge had long departed this 'mortal coil' and no one was aware of any of the details of the charge attached to this estate. The amount was small and I offered to get things moving by paying the now trifling sum listed. Of course, this was not a legal answer. Adverts were placed in newspapers to try to locate the person who raised the charge or those now in control of this estate. Fortunately for the deal, no one came forward and the courts agreed to remove the charge. If it had turned out differently and someone came forward to be paid, it would have been a considerable sum due to the effect of compounding interest. Once something is attached to a deed there is significant action needed to have it removed regardless of the duration.

Lien.

If your lawyer advises you that a 'lien' is registered against the title this should not cause you much concern. This is an encumbrance (usually a debt) that is recorded on the title and 'runs with the land'. There are a number of types of lien and they are named dependent on who registered the debt. The lien will be removed on payment and the encumbrance is cancelled from the title. Your lawyer will ensure that all outstanding liens are satisfied at closing and the land is transferred with the liens removed. If the term 'lis pendens' is used it means that a lawsuit has been filed in relation to the property title. Obvious advice: consult with your lawyer before you move forward.

Conditions and Restrictions.

Your lawyer may well raise legal issues around access to the lot. It can be that a roadway leading to the lot is over someone else's ground or it is unclear who specifically owns the ground or accessway. Or conversely, someone potentially has a right of way across your lot.

It is often difficult to assess how large or insignificant this problem may turn out.

The other issue is, you are buying today but may at some future point be a seller. How will your purchaser view the situation? In these cases, discuss taking out an insurance policy to remedy a perceived problem. The seller may well undertake to meet the (usually) one-off cost.

The second issue that may be raised is over permits. Lawyers are legal advisors, not planning specialists and so perhaps discuss the issue and ramifications with a professional planning consultant.

Lenders often require that purchaser's take out title insurance as a protection against title issues becoming a point of contention at some future time. This is to protect both the lenders and purchaser.

A developer in the truest sense develops one thing into another. By understanding the rules, this can work in your favor. As has often been said, you should 'be thinking about the day you sell on the day you buy'.

Purchase Agreement

This is the stage where both parties sign the purchase and sale contract. The seller and purchaser are both legally bound to honour this agreement and it will clearly state the penalties if either party withdraws for any reason. The law society or real estate institute in your state or province provides lists of questions the seller must complete on the contract form, including signing legal statements of what is offered for sale and the seller's knowledge of any neighbourhood disputes, locations of boundaries and existence of easements.

The concern to the purchaser during the 'before contract exchange' period is if the deal falters and does not proceed or someone else makes a higher offer. To move matters along, both sides can agree to sign contracts subject to later title searches not revealing problems. This can only be agreed by careful legal wording as disputes should be avoided wherever possible. The prudent way forward is to wait until you have full information before any commitments are made.

An agreed deposit is normally paid by the purchaser. This is usually in the 5-10% range of the total purchase price, although this can be varied by mutual agreement.

Chained transactions can be stressful. This is where a chain is formed of people not only buying but also selling. What no-one wants is to sell and settle before they have purchased, as then they would potentially be homeless! Your lawyer will guide you through this process.

Know Your Client (KYC).

Your lawyer has to confirm where your funds are coming from. This may seem odd but governments are checking on this to cut out money laundering through property from the proceeds of crime. If they are not satisfied, they are legally bound to inform the authorities of any suspicions they have.

Further than this, advisors and lending institutions are legally obliged to follow strict government criteria and reporting procedures. They are mandated to inform the appropriate authorities of all transactions over certain minimum limits, whether or not they have any reason to be doubtful of the origin of the funds.

Closing

Completion happens at a set time after agreeing the purchase and normally ranges between fourteen days and six weeks. Your lawyer will carry out some final checks just to ensure all matters are OK, but generally they will rely on the searches provided.

The buyer will pay the following on closing:

- The balance of the agreed sale price
- Any bank attorney's fee if a mortgage has been arranged
- Any applicable mortgage recording tax
- Buyer and lender premiums for title insurance tax
- Any other lender fees
- Any applicable state special transfer taxes

On completion, the money is paid to the seller and the purchaser takes possession. Your lawyer has to ensure your details are properly registered on the title deeds with the municipality clerk's office and all the relevant documents are complete. This ensures you have full title to the property and all is recorded in the local town hall.

Mortgages and Finance.

Mortgages are normally drawn down as capital repayment loans. Your financial advisor and broker should advise you on the most appropriate product for you. Lawyers are not allowed to make decisions. This does not mean they will not advise you and outline options, but in the end they can only act on your instructions. It is worthwhile to carefully listen to their advice as they are part of your team of consultants and are offering advice to legally protect you.

Auctions and Contracts.

Auctions are where matters can go very wrong. Purchasing at auction instantly puts you into a legal exchange of contract to purchase. In most jurisdictions, buyers do not get a cooling off period and therefore you don't get a chance to show the documents to your legal team or your designer/planner. So if you purchase on a whim while standing at an auction, you have not had due diligence carried out on your purchase: nonetheless you are legally obliged to comply with the contract or forgo your deposit.

The upside? Auctions can produce property bargains, or for the seller, sometimes they achieve sales above the market rate. The sensible way of purchasing at auction is to plan.

Set a watch list to follow properties in your preferred areas as they come onto the market. Make it your business to get to know the salespeople at the different estate agencies and ask them to let you know as properties come onto the market. If an interesting property comes up, ask if they think the seller will accept an offer before the auction date.

When potential properties come up, ask your lawyer to review the legal pack and ask your designer/planner to review the planning status. They will probably charge you for this even if you decide not to purchase or are unsuccessful purchasing on the day.

Paying for advice that doesn't culminate in purchasing a lot can be an expensive hobby, but it can be a lot cheaper than ending up with an unsuitable property.

TRUE STORY

> I once saw a property for sale at auction listed as having a planning permit for a largeish home. When we looked at the site, it seemed like a lot of home on the lot. We took a few dimensions and confirmed the house as drawn would not fit within the boundary and in fact spilled over into the neighbor's yard. We thought this was odd and looked at the drawings as shown on the planner's website and indicated as approved. The dimensions were as shown (incorrectly) and to compound matters a window that was indicated in the sale particulars was not shown on the permit drawings. Never take anything for granted; go back to approved drawings not those sent to you by a seller or their representative.

Caveat emptor is a Latin phrase which sums up the end point of any land purchase – 'buyer beware'. Once you are in contract, you have to pay to get out. Plus, after completion of the sale you are in the position of having to go to law for redress, without any guarantee of success.

Money.

At completion of the purchase, you must have your finances in place. If you do not, you could well be in breach of contract and subject to penalties. Eventually, you could lose the deposit. You have signed a binding contract and all parties are expected to fulfil their obligations.

Interstate Purchase.

If you are buying land in the US without visiting the plots interstate the transaction may come under the Interstate Land Sales Full Disclosure Act (ILSA). This is under the control Consumer Financial Protection Bureau (CFPB). The purpose is to prevent fraudulent property schemes preying on the unwary purchaser. If you are purchasing in a state, you do not reside in, you may need to discuss the procedures with your lawyer.

Chapter 4 – Action

- Set a 'watch list' to follow properties in your preferred area
- Listen to what your lawyer is saying
- Get your finances in order before completion day
- Think about the day you sell as well as the day you buy

CHAPTER 5
SUMMARY

You are one player in a list of a dozen players who affect your development. Do they care as much as you… or do they even care at all?

Highlights covered in this chapter include:

- Name check and responsibilities of all the players
- Fitzpatrick rating awarded to each player
- You are the 'King Pin' in the build process but do not expect any recognition

CHAPTER 5

THE PLAYERS

'You'll Never Walk Alone'.
— Rogers and Hammerstein

The Rogers and Hammerstein song 'You'll Never Walk Alone' could have been composed with the owner-builder in mind. The term suggests a solitary activity but nothing is further from the truth. Construction is a true team activity. Parts and people interact all the time and positive contributions make all the difference.

All are important and all have a say in what you do. They are 'interested parties', unrelated to each other, but all converging over your activities. They play a part in how you proceed and what materials your completed home will comprise of, how energy efficient it is and how it will look. All in all, the players are important in your world.

However, they only care about their service in isolation from all the other players. They care in differing amounts about you, the single output point of the whole exercise. As far as they are concerned, they exist to complete their function regardless of your outcome. In essence, they are there to do their thing; not to worry about your thing!

As you are the only single point, they all come to, you can compartmentalise them while also seeing the full picture. Recognizing who the players are in your owner-build world allows you to ensure they are all considered. You must smooth their way to make it easy for them to assist you to deliver the project.

TRUE STORY

> A wealthy guy I know had sold his business and was retiring. He had architects draw up plans for a new home and obtain a planning permit. He announced that he and his family were off on a world cruise and it was the architect's job to have the building complete and the house furnished on their return in eight months' time. The architects called him the 'perfect client' as he would not interfere with their work. He returned and was distressed to find that works were not nearly complete and he had to lease a local house to have somewhere to live. What the 'team' had not factored in were all the decisions that need to be taken as works progressed and the importance of the client/team relationship. He got stuck in as client, and the building was completed after a further eight months. (We were merely observers).

Your build journey will be populated by players representing many different organizations and bodies that you will engage, consult, have certify, regulate and facilitate your building work; all of whom you must pay. They are made up of 12 sets of players, all playing for their own teams. As organizations they cover a wide range of services, nonetheless they all impact on your build and all must be managed. Following is this so-called 'Dirty Dozen'.

The Dirty Dozen

- Owner, Owner-Builder and Project Manager
- Key Design Professionals
- Secondary Design Professionals
- Suppliers
- Contractors/Builders/Subs
- Building Inspectors and Certifiers
- Infrastructure and Utility Companies
- Insurance Companies
- Professional/Trade Associations
- Government Bodies
- Financial Institutions/Brokers
- Legal and Regulatory Consultants

This is the point where your professional team has to be named. You must consider the makeup of the group who advise you and who you consult with.

The difference between advice and consult is: *advice* is given and can be taken or discarded. *Consult* means to seek opinions and counsel, to deliberate and confer with someone.

It's time to define how you will deliver the project from now until completion.

The question is : *who are 'The Players' and how much are they involved?*

Fitzpatrick Score

To assess what responsibility, they take – as opposed to how much influence they exert – I devised the Fitzpatrick Score. You care how they perform but do they care how you and your project perform? What level of involvement do they have in your project? The highest involvement level is set at 10/10, with the lowest 0/10.

Owner, Owner-Builder and Project Manager.

No work would happen if an owner did not step forward and seek to build something. In this case, it is a house and you are the construction manager and perhaps an operative as well. You have your own reasons for starting this task, but regardless of what they are, you and you alone will be responsible for the outcome. You are funding the project through loans and guarantees from lenders. This is not 'other people's money'; it is your money and you'll be liable to repay every cent, plus a few more for interest!

So, you must define things carefully for others. You will develop the concept alongside the designers and provide input on the end users' requirements. How many bedrooms, what size kitchen, etc. By agreeing the scope of work, you are projecting a certain quality of finish and character. You will decide on any extra environmental features or standards over and above those required by building codes and regulations.

This all leads to the scheduling of budgets, placement of orders and entering into contracts.

You have a clear stake in the success of the project.

Fitzpatrick Score 10/10

Key Design Professionals.

The key design professionals are the architect or designer, town planner, structural engineer and possibly surveyor or cost engineer. They will assist in the development by working towards the goals laid out by the program. They will advise on the look and implementation of the works, even assisting with sequencing, particularly for structural matters. They will propose products and look to set a tone that lines up with the proposed budgets. This will lead to building permit applications, and the production of working drawings and specifications.

As they are *key*, it is important the selected professionals are people you can work with and trust.

Fitzpatrick Score 7/10

Secondary Design Professionals.

These secondary professionals are often introduced by the key professionals. They carry out specific set tasks and are not involved in the project's overall process. Their role is a specialist one, for example, surveyors setting out the work, consulting on 'rights of light' or boundary wall matters.

One anomaly in the professionals is the town or urban planning consultant. Their work can be intense but is usually finished before actual construction work commences.

The big picture is, the secondary designers do their job, issue an invoice and then withdraw.

Fitzpatrick Score 4/10

Suppliers.

I know a supplier who is very good at their job. If you want intricate advice on the right screw for the right job, the right lock for any given door, you are in the right place at their store. They have a prominent sign displayed behind the counter (yes, counters still exist) which boldly states:

> *'Because something is an emergency for you,*
> *it does not mean it is an emergency for us'.*

It's hardly a positive, culturally sensitive message to send to your clients who are used to politically correct speech. They do however tell a truth - they will help, but they will not do the work for you. Give them sufficient notice and they will help you select the material and arrange a timely delivery.

The owner-builder has to predict what is wanted and where it fits into the program. A good specialist contractor or supplier will almost be a design-and-build specialist, they are experts in their trade and will share their experience with you. Listen carefully to what they say and enquire what they need to make things right in their world. They provide high quality products and they care that their products reach you in first class condition and on time. After that point you are on your own.

If you make their life easy, it will rebound and make your life easy.

Fitzpatrick Score 2/10

Contractors/Builders/Subs.

They are the most difficult bunch to categorize. They can become part of the family and be seen as 'gems' that are passed onto people you care about or they can be the embodiment of a natural disaster. They can have skills that leave you amazed and produce what you consider is akin to a fine art installation or perhaps come up short. They are however, the group that you get closest to. All you can do is treat them well while they are on your project and hope they return the compliment.

For contractors, one important way of helping them is to prepare the work areas as they want it and ready to go. By working *with* contractors, you are not working against them.

Fitzpatrick Score 7/10

Building Inspectors and Certifiers.

Building inspectors and certifiers are directed and constrained by codes and regulations. If you co-operate and build everything to code, all well and good; they will be pleased to see work proceed safely and properly. They will usually engage in conversation and listen to reason and argument. On the other hand, they will not be happy if they suspect shortcuts and they think you are trying to game the system.

Inspectors/Certifiers are there to sign off work that comply with the regulations and code. If you do not co-operate and meet the code, they are not overly concerned. Their world will continue much as it is and they will not be at all stressed. They will simply issue non-compliance notices and refuse to pass the home as complete or habitable. This will impact on your insurance and almost certainly void any guarantees. The municipality may then issue compliance notices for you to rectify work. This will upset your lender and not be a good place to start a conversation about extending your loan. It is, of course, entirely your call.

Fitzpatrick Score 2/10

> **TRUE STORY**
>
> Many inspectors and contractors love to chat about disasters they have seen. My personally witnessed favorite is a toilet bowl fitted within a shower enclosure. Not in a wet room but within the area the shower nozzle sprays water and is enclosed by the shower screens. The intention was to share the drain outlet! If you look through trade magazines, you will see examples sent in as hilarious tales by readers. There is a more serious element to all this entertainment. These 'funny' and reckless installations are actually dangerous and were presumably installed by professionals. Ensure you do not become the talk of the area!

Infrastructure and Utility Companies.

Infrastructure/Utility companies often have a monopoly on the supply of their services with strict application processes which are to be faithfully followed or you will not get your service. Sometimes just faithfully following the rules is not even enough, as your project seems the last thing on their collective minds. For them, the customer can be ignored and an apology for delay just seems an impossible dream.

The only bright light is often the person who comes out to do the work. They are usually engaged and know their stuff. Treat them well and they will often respond in kind.

The constant with these companies is to be scrupulous with your record keeping and always get a name and job reference from them at every contact. This will help your project, at some future point, to be found in the system.

As power/water/sewerage/telco authorities are regulated by government, they report publicly on complaint numbers and produce statistics on customer satisfaction.

Fitzpatrick Score 1/10

Insurance Companies.

You need insurance, as the penalty of not being insured is too great when a serious issue arises. They care if you make a claim and are pleased if you do not. Responsible to their stakeholders and board, they are not directly engaged with your project and are on hand if disaster strikes.

Fitzpatrick Score 0/10

> **TIP BOX**
>
> The owner-builder cannot be expected to keep up with changes to law at its source, but you can subscribe to owner-build magazines covering your area or region. Look out for articles which translate these updates into ordinary language. Hardware stores often distribute free supplier magazines, which also cover good practice and building inspection changes.
>
> Professional consultants try to keep up with continuing professional development within their field, although sometimes matters slip past them. If an article you've read seems to imply a change has occurred that affects you, do not be shy in forwarding the article to one of your team of consultants for their input. If this is done in the spirit of mutual assistance, this helps you meet new regulations as they appear.

Professional/Trade Associations.

These fall into two categories. The first for members of the profession you appoint and the second you yourself can join.

The first has the rights and objectives of their members at heart, not their members' clients. For example, Royal Architectural Institute of Canada (RAIC) or National Association of Home Builders (NAHB) can be somewhat useful, with search lists and standard forms for engaging their members on your project. The associations always look to promote the professional standing of their members within the industry and in the broader community. They can require their members to safeguard the public by having current insurances and standards of conduct. You can make complaints to professional associations, although the results are mixed.

The second category are associations you can join, like *Build Your House Yourself University (BYHUY)* or one of the many owner-building websites. These can be useful as they publish member-only magazines, arrange meetings and online talks, podcasts, etc. This can be useful when you have a query best answered by a 'brother in arms' on the web.

Both categories of associations are there to serve their members and make representations to government departments, including public enquiries on behalf of their members. They do not have a stake in your project and are not interested in specifics.

Fitzpatrick Score 0/10

Government Bodies.

The government produces laws, rules and codes and levy development taxes. These building codes are administered by states, provinces, local government, building inspectors, and planning departments. The one thing all governments excel at is producing new laws and changing existing ones. In planning departments, sometimes you do come across planning officers who like to see fine designs brought forward, but as an institution they are not affected by your progress. As a body they are impervious to your time constraints.

Fitzpatrick Score 0/10

Financial Institutions/Brokers.

Brokers.

You may be involved with middlemen, such as brokers, who advise on finance and maintain strong links and contacts with potential lenders. These people are friendlier than the lender and are in a direct relationship with you, particularly as they only get a fee if they successfully negotiate a deal on your behalf. They only deal with you to facilitate your original loan and do not re-enter your life as part of this project.

Lenders.

They are in your world because you need finance and they lend money. They do care about their investment and will usually instruct a surveyor to monitor your progress. Their surveyors value your applications for regular drawdowns to allow you to complete the project. You pay them for this survey service that protects their investment. They care abstractly, and will be inconvenienced if you run into financial difficulty. Lenders do not like owner-builders coming back for increased sums and will be wary if you cannot meet your objectives and targets. Lenders themselves are coming under increasing scrutiny from the media and governments, who believe many failings in past national economies were due to poor lending practices. They have countered this with increased compliance, which means more hurdles between you and the funding. As they have a financial interest, they do care, as they stand to lose by you not succeeding.

Fitzpatrick Score 5/10

Legal and Regulatory Consultants.

At the early stages, you will get legal advice from lawyers around purchasing issues, and at the end you must ensure all taxes are properly paid or reclaimed. Governments may have refund opportunities for taxes paid around the land purchase or material purchase for owner-builders. Lawyers and accountants are often the go-to people during the project over many issues and can often reassure you over your eligibility and the possible lodgement of claims.

A good lawyer and accountant are very useful team members.

Fitzpatrick Score 7/10

What can You Do to Engage as Effectively as You Can?

The three things you can to do are monitor, recognize options and reschedule. You need to keep across all the outstanding decisions and *who is where* on the schedule of works. The car industry has 'just in time' material supply procedures; the owner-builder has 'just get it done' procedures. Until a task is complete, something else cannot commence. This is too much to carry about in your head and so you must commit this information to forms and follow processes. This is best achieved in a neat, simple system, allowing you to clearly explain what has to be done.

A visual illustration in the form of a *schedule of work* is required, to monitor all these different actions. Monitoring is not the only focus; seeing viable options and knowing when to move from one work point to another, or reschedule the work so progress is maintained, is key.

Overall, you and the other players (all directly or indirectly) have a hand in what happens and what is constructed on your piece of land. They all know their part and what input they expect to offer within the process. They design, they install, they bring forward rules to carefully follow, they finance and they underwrite disasters. But only one player really cares: the owner-builder!

Without this role, and his commitment, all the others are simply producing *squiggles on a page*.

Recognition.

When it comes to recognition, the builder/project manager is way down the line. I challenge you to think of the most identifiable modern building in your city or area and look it up on a web-based search engine. I did this and was told straightaway who the architect was. An outline was given over the construction method utilized. They said this was a 'first' in this country and that 'path-breaking engineering methods were used'. Not a word about the people who actually did the work and made sense of what was asked of them.

The builder took the designs and proved they were affordable. Made sure they would stand up and meet building code. They cleared the site, removing dangerous materials, and safely planned material deliveries using complex computer schedules for construction work to meet time constraints and labor availability. They instructed and supervised the work, looking at quality control and site OH&S. They thought about maintenance of the components and produced ongoing maintenance plans. They tested and certified installations and met the requirements of outside bodies over access and fire safety, etc. Overall, they made a space people could reside in, use for recreation or business. They delivered the project from the bottom to the top. All this, with little public recognition. If anything, there seems a generally held belief that this work is not an important role in society.

This is not the case in manufacturing of aeroplanes and their engines, where the manufacturer who brings the designers, engineers and skilled operatives together is lauded.

Fitzpatrick Score

Fitzpatrick Score for Involvement and Commitment	Maximum	Awarded
Owner/Owner-Builder/Project Manager	10	10
Key Design Professionals	10	8
Secondary Design Professionals	10	5
Suppliers	10	2
Contractors/Builders/Subs	10	7
Building Inspectors and Certifiers	10	2
Infrastructure and Utility Companies	10	1
Professional/Trade Associations	10	0
Insurance Companies	10	0
Financial Institutions/Brokers	10	5
Government Bodies	10	0
Legal and Regulatory Consultants	10	7
Total	120	47
Combined points awarded to all the 'Players' 47 out of a possible 120		

It seems to me, only three players positively care and are committed to your project. Others care about the success of their involvement inasmuch as they take pride in their work and want you to be successful enough to pay their invoice. Perhaps this is a little unfair to the players you meet along the way who gel with the owner-builder and become *real* team members.

The players involved total 12. If you take yourself out of the equation, it leaves 11, which makes a possible maximum score of 110 points for players involved in your project. The Fitzpatrick score is given as 32 for the remaining players combined. In terms of caring, you are way out in front, lighting the way.

The Players

Owner/Self-Builder	Key Professionals	Secondary Design Professionals
You	Architect	Setting Out Engineer
Your Named Team	Structural Engineer	Geotechnical Engineer
	Planning Consultant	Party Wall Surveyor
	PQS (Cost Engineer)	Services/Heating Consultants
		Plus others as required

Suppliers	Contractors	Building Inspection
Windows & Doors	Carpenters	Government/Municipal Authority
Kitchen	Plumbers	Statutory Bodies
Bricks	Bricklayers	Utility Providers
Flooring	Concreter	Regulations & Codes
Structural Steel	Roofing	
Concrete	Plus all trades	
Plus all Materials		

Infrastructure and Utility Companies	Government Bodies	Insurance Companies
Electricity	Central	Building Insurance
Gas	Local / State	Public Liability
Telephone/Cable	Planners	Materials & Theft
Water	Tax Office	Building Warranty Insurer
Sewerage		Tools/Equipment

Professional Trade Associations	Finance	Legal & Regulatory Consultants
Architects Registration Board	Bank/Mortgage Company	Lawyers/Solicitors
Engineers Professional Association	Family	Accountants
Builders Associations etc.	Brokers	

TRUE STORY

I saw a story in a newspaper regarding an upset in one of the most 'exclusive' neighbourhoods. The 'celebrity' residents were complaining of building works continuing on a substantial property for 7 years with no end in sight to the noise, dust and deliveries. This seemed like a very slow build and I remembered that I knew a contractor who was working for the named and shamed popular singer-songwriter who was indicated as the owner. When I next saw the contractor, I asked him what the story was.

It seemed that the owner was having too much fun to want the works to complete. When things were finished, he instructed they be taken down and reconfigured with a new design. He got on well with the workforce, even joining them for meal breaks and becoming 'one of the guys'.

People look for different things from the players and as with all matters having a plan to follow will definitely focus your vision.

This owner lacked vision but was wealthy enough to indulge himself, and if he chose to continuously live in a building site, I suppose he got what he wanted!

What is it you want from the players or 'Dirty Dozen'? By tracking each one and offering an appropriate approach, you can get the result you deserve.

Chapter 5 – Action

- Engage with all the players
- Prepare a schedule of work
- Monitor their performance
- Focus on what you want from them

CHAPTER 6
SUMMARY

Your consultants are the people who will deliver your project and bring their expertise to the team. There are many professionals available and it is important you know who you need.

Highlights covered in this chapter include:

- What roles do you want consultants to have in your build?
- Can you instruct consultants by stages?
- Do you have the right to separately use their drawings?
- Information, communication and hard work
- Is insurance important?
- Review project milestones

CHAPTER 6

THE PROFESSIONALS – CONSULTANTS AND TRADESPEOPLE

'Make each day your masterpiece'.
– John Wooden

Consultants are an intricate part of the owner-build experience. No-one knows everything and has experience of every part of construction. Perhaps you feel this is not the case and you can do it all, but the rest of us need specialist assistance. By wise use of consultants, we can produce something special.

Organizing Yourself

The key to successful owner-building is organization. To effectively succeed, you must clearly understand what you are trying to achieve and how you will get there. You must project manage not only for yourself but also all the players involved.

This starts at the very beginning. Every project needs a champion who cares passionately about delivery and success. Someone has to step forward and take responsibility. From then on, it is about information, communication and sheer hard work.

Information.

There are a large number of consultants you can call upon to assist you with your designs and calculations. You will not need them all; in fact, some of the consultants will multi-task and take over more than one role.

Consultants like to be clear on their roles and may list services you can pick and choose from. Yet, consultants will not build the home for you; they will design what you should carry out. The responsibility is firmly on the owner-builder to construct properly. If it is not built as per the design then there are major implications.

Because of this, clear and concise information is required. If you don't understand what they are designing for you, how can you build it? Do not be afraid to ask questions and get into the details. Consultants are usually very helpful in this way and are generally pleased you are keen enough to listen and be involved in the whole process.

You want them to come up with wonderful designs and give timely advice to assist you to construct your home. So, the place to start is by appointing the principal designer. This is a vital appointment and one not to be taken lightly. You should set a scope for what it is you actually want, not perhaps what they offer.

What the designer wants is… a high-quality design, wonderfully meeting your needs as they perceive them and matching the essence of your program. What you want is… all of this, plus an actual planning permit granted and a project that meets your budget.

You know a refused permission will delay matters and cost real money. The designer knows this as well and does not benefit from a refusal. But it is your money in the game.

Perhaps you can propose to merge your interests. Rather than appoint the designer for the project, appoint them up until the granting of planning permission. This can be classed a stage appointment, where on the achievement of the stage, a payment becomes due. This can be on a fixed sum, so all parties know where they stand.

What happens if planning is refused? Do you still make the full payment?

> ## TRUE STORY
>
> Hope
>
> I know an architect who had a difficult situation in his office. He had worked on lot designs for a client developing a house proposal. The house plan was refused a permit by the municipality and matters remained there.
>
> The client marketed the land for sale without permission but with the 'aura' of potential, which led to hope by an inexperienced purchaser.
>
> The new owner, after purchase, was distraught to discover from the architect that the site had little hope of receiving a building permit. In tears, he confided that he was intending to build a home for his frail elderly father. This useless purchase had lost all his available money. His father would never have the home his son so wanted him to have.
>
> Had he or his professional team investigated properly before purchase and not afterwards, this could have been avoided.

Communication.

When you receive information, you must share it. Drawings will probably be sent by e-mail, making it easy to send on to all interested contractors and suppliers. Never let anyone work off old information, as it becomes confusing on-site and leads to mistakes. If a printer is available, print off hard copies on the largest sheets of paper you can. When you are working on site on a critical detail, print off sheets and hand them out to the workers.

It's wise to laminate a set of the latest plans at the appropriate scale and place them on-site for general use. The information on the final drawings is important and needs to be preserved. Lamination will avoid damage through rough handling or getting wet. The operatives also appreciate clear and accessible information as it makes their lives easier. Keep an eye out on the site and collect and remove any out-of-date or revised plans.

I also copy or print off typical details and building regulations of how things should be put together. If you approach the on-site contractors in a helpful manner, this should not cause any upset. If they intend to construct otherwise and not in the method recommended, this should be agreed.

These days, many contractors and operatives own smart phones and pads/tablets, so these details can also be electronically sent. The important issue is that we are all working to the same details.

Leadership.

People follow leaders who are decisive and ready to take charge, but only if they are talking sense. It's your job to be in control of details because in the owner-build world, all details matter. As mentioned elsewhere, the cross-over points between trades are where most issues arise. It is the place where misunderstandings blossom.

People are very sociable and respond quickly to others and to the atmospheres created. Studies at Georgetown University show that even 15-minutes in someone's company can change perceptions and attitudes. We all want our home to be well built and a positive 'can do' attitude will push this forward. We all co-operate better and work to higher standards when everyone around us is doing the same. All on-site projects have a personality, and it's your job to make it a hard-working and responsible personality which thrives when progress is achieved and works are going well.

Insurance.

If a structural failure occurs at some point after completion, it's less worrying for you as all your consultants should carry design insurance. This will cover the loss, if it can be demonstrated the failure is a result of their design. If you build faithfully to their design, their insurers should cover you. If you do not, you will not be covered, regardless of opinions on the appropriateness of their design.

If you want to make design changes, seek confirmation and approval/agreement from the relevant consultant, prior to the changes, bring made.

If you do take action and make a claim, it is easier to get it through if your insurance company act for you in the matter. You should not rely on a third party's insurance company as they may make things difficult, meaning money will be spent long before a decision and possible costs are awarded. Your insurance policy should be standalone and any claims should be made through your insurers.

In some areas, insurance is mandatory, but even where it is not, many owner-build their home within a longer-term insurance scheme. Schemes can be included as part of the building inspection process. The longer-term insurance, which can be passed onto successive owners, is often for a 6 to 10-year period. If it transpires you have not followed the approved design, this insurance coverage is at risk.

For example, all new homes constructed in Ontario, Canada must have a seven year statutory warranty insurance. Owner-builders must register their project and obtain a Letter of Confirmation and become responsible for the warranty coverage. If you do not follow the regulations, you are liable to prosecution and so follow the local requirements in your area.

All consultants offer a service to provide advice and design to clients, and as such, a wide number of people can be tasked to carry out roles. It is the owner-builder's responsibility to appoint an appropriate team of consultants. Often consultants recommend other professionals they respect, but the responsibility lays with the client.

The best approach is to recruit team members who fit your project. Do not be afraid to check if your proposed consultant has carried out similar works to your project. Most consultants proudly advertise past projects on their websites and these projects can often be an indicator of style, if not substance.

As with 'The Program', you must be clear on how you will build your team and who will take responsibility for specific tasks and outcomes. Traditionally the architect has acted as contract administrator within the building team. As such, you may seek their advice on your particular circumstances.

What Do Professional & Trade Associations Do?

Professional & Trade Associations like to encourage a positive view of their members, who they promote as the preferred choice for an appointment on a construction project. They encourage their members to regularly improve their knowledge through continuing professional development programs.

Many professional associations act as a safeguard to the public as they insist members are insured and so will not leave clients let-down and without redress. They also enforce codes of conduct and remove members from the association if their reported performance dips below minimum standards.

Some professional associations limit full memberships to candidates who can demonstrate competence through examination, experience and interview, while other trade associations simply require a signed statement and a fee. Therefore, each one should be looked at in isolation and assessed as to the relevance to your project. All professionally-qualified consultants are certainly not identical in quality of work and design, but membership does indicate a minimum level of competence.

Lenders and other institutions often put a lot of store in key members of your consultants' team being a member of certain prestigious professional associations. They want to assure themselves of your consultants' competence and see this as a further risk reduction for them, since they are funding the project. Lenders may well ask for evidence of consultants' insurances and indemnities. Even if they do not, you should check your consultants carry current Professional Indemnity (PI) insurance.

Your Design Team

Your team will always be the people who can add most to your chances of success.

Planner (Town/Urban Planner).

I started with the planner so this role is not overshadowed by the designer.

Many designers, particularly architects, are doubtful whether planners can give much assistance on a single house project. Architects often see their role as designing a home to meet your program and delivering the project through the permit process.

Planners see things from a different perspective. They are not there to hold your hand and discuss the size of your garage; they are there to get your project approved and issued with a building permit.

One Job. Only One Job.

The good planners like to marshal all the other consultants into focusing on this point. If they can, they like to chair discussions and talk over policy and local plans. They will also slip 'sleeper' points into the application in order to resurrect them later in case of a refusal of the permit. These points are reserved to use at the appeal stage as evidence of the failure of the planner to take all relevant matters into account.

Planners will discuss and give guidance over issues, such as: what roof heights will be acceptable, appropriate window positions and overlooking issues with neighbors, etc.

So, all in all, you can see why some designers think planners overstep the mark and try to take over.

Planners are most useful when dealing with contentious sites, where layers of restrictions and local heritage issues are plentiful. They can assist by rebutting points raised and give comprehensive 'legalistic' answers to most questions. Importantly, as they are closer to bureaucrats than designers, they are not tied to the concept of your design and can more impartially advise on strategies to meet planning challenges.

They are particularly useful if you wish to subdivide a site to accommodate more than a single dwelling, or if you want a mixed use, such as residence and work (aka Live/Work). Some people like an office and a home at the same location. If this is your intention, you need to check whether a mixed used permit is likely to be issued.

Architects/Designers.

It is usual for an owner-builder to consult a designer. Architects are commonly thought of as the most qualified designers. In almost all areas of the world, architects are registered professionals with a strict code of conduct and registration. They guard their status as the senior professional consultant.

One thing you are not often told: you can instruct your house designer on a stage-by-stage basis. The stages are not a secret; it's just knowing where to look for the information.

Architects' registration boards provide information on the main stages of instruction/ appointment. In summary, they are usually as follows:

Stage 1	Initial Design and Program
Stage 2	Permit and Application Submission
Stages 3-4	Technical Design to Bidding
Stages 5-6	Construction to Completion

An architect or designer can assist you to prepare your building application and will often submit the application on your behalf. This is the point where you need a completed design and a comprehensive application with assistance from secondary consultants to achieve building permit.

After planning, you will decide on the process of delivering your build. It can be anything from a traditional bidding process for trades through to you carrying out every task personally, or as much as you are allowed to by building codes/regulations.

The next decision is what level of information you require to carry out the build. Architects and designers like to produce full working drawings for all aspects of the build. Perhaps this is a perfect reflection of what you want, or it may be that you want technical design information only to meet building permit approval. Or you could be somewhere in between.

This is an important issue, as it is a real cost point. For example, a designer producing drawings for the millwork subcontractor to produce hand-built wardrobes, with runners procured from obscure parts of the world, may be ideal or it may be unnecessary.

Some like to continue a winning, working relationship with a trusted design partner and confidant. Others will take the 'fancy' design and ask a draftsperson or surveyor to 'work up' the building permit approval issues in a standard 'technician' way.

One point to be sure of is: who has the copyright of the design and drawings? If you are thinking of taking the *design and the drawings* to a technician, then you will need the designers to agree and give permission. If it was *not* agreed for others to use the drawings, then you may have an issue utilizing 'your' drawings. You can keep the design, but the others will, completely from scratch, reproduce the design as their own.

A breach of copyright occurs when one person uses another person's drawings to produce further drawings where no express consent from the copyright holder has been provided. But copying is not an essential element of a potential breach. If you employed a designer and paid them, then you can build the house on that property to that design without infringing the copyright. If you construct a house to this design at a different location, then you are infringing copyright. If you are at all concerned by this, seek legal advice.

Cost Engineer (CE).

A cost engineer (CE) aka a quantity surveyor (PQS) can work well for some owner-builders. This team member comes into his own if you intend to contract out roles by competitive bids. The CE will initially provide budget advice before your planning application is submitted. This will assist you and the designer to make early decisions over the layout and size of the property.

After planning permission is granted, the CE can prepare a specification of work and calculate a detailed cost plan for the project. She will prepare specification documents for tender purposes to be issued to contractors and suppliers, ensuring all contractors receive identical information.

If you do approach a CE, what is it you want from the specification?

For a single house, there is basically a choice of two levels of information usually required:

- Project Specification
- Project Specification with Quantities

Project Specifications is a document stating in detail which works are to be undertaken and separating them into trades. It then goes further and breaks down each section into an itemised account of the works. These comprise separate schedules for each trade, including descriptions of each component of the work and the associated required standards that must be met. These standards are usually expressed as national building regulations or codes of practice.

Project Specification with Quantities is virtually the same document but with quantities attached. The quantities are useful because if you are carrying out the works, it gives you an idea of the material quantities required and so helps with pricing.

If you are seeking competitive quotations from more than one specialist contractor, quantities are useful for the following reasons:

- The contractor will not need to spend time calculating the amount of material required, as you are asking him to base his quotation on the amounts you provide. This is easier for him and he can simply apply rates to your information.

- When you receive more than one quotation, it is easier for you to assess 'like for like' quotations. Specialist contractors will often *not* do exactly as you ask. Rather than provide you with an easy to understand, individually priced format, they will group items together and merge items under a single price for their own various reasons.
- It is important to establish if all the items in your specification are included. What appeared at first as a competitive price could in fact be the most expensive option.
- Specifications allow you to confirm the extent of the included works. If the specialist contractor compiles their own quotation, they may not include all the items you and the design team wanted. This is a common area of misunderstanding and is only completely avoided by clear agreements before the order is placed.
- If one of the specialist contractors raises a query on your information or requires clarification, try to resolve the query. If you can, reference the clarification to a building standard or regulation. The PQS will be able to assist. If appropriate, update the other contractors, with the same information, to assist them to prepare their quotations.

> **TIP BOX**
>
> ### Avoiding Disagreements
>
> A priced set of specifications will be a document you can return to. It is prudent to include a copy of the relevant pages as priced by the contractor as part of your order. This specification document confirms what work component and quantities are allowed for within the price.
>
> It's common for the scope of the works to vary and so this document becomes the set point of agreement. If any component of work is omitted or altered, it can be deducted from the specifications and if a component is added, it can be increased in line with the prices quoted in the specification. This aids resolution when the final accounts for a specialist contractor are agreed.
>
> A contractor is only committed to carry out the scope of work at the quoted rate *up to the level of quantities provided*. If for example, a mistake was made and he has under-priced an item, you can only 'reasonably' insist the specified quantity is carried out at the quoted rate. Excess or additional work after the quantity has been exceeded can be varied at a newly agreed rate.

- Priced specifications are a good starting point during negotiation with a specialist contractor if you seek a fixed price from them; i.e. an 'all-in-one deal' or lump sum. It allows them to take a view on the complexity of the work and come up with an overall, not-to-be-exceeded price, as long as you do not vary the scope of work. This gives you security over cost variations.

The CE can also advise you on contractual points. How do you formalise your orders? Do they relate to a contract or a procedure? The CE will understand all forms of contract and therefore advise when you should formally enter into a contract and when it is simply not worthwhile.

If you decide to seek bids from builders for the whole project, the CE can prepare your bidding documents and assist you to adjudicate the bids. She can also value the regular applications made by the builder as work proceeds and advise on cost projections, and more importantly, overruns.

Roof Coverings Specification

<u>Roof Coverings and Rooflights as Drawing H8644 - 8 of 8 Issue A</u> <u>Roofs - R2.0 plus double sided foil (blanket or foil and insulation</u> <u>Roof Coverings - The House</u> <u>Colourbond Windspray Sheet Roof Coverings; sarking felt; timber battens 3" Climafoam tongued and grooved XPS Insulation Board; double sided blanket of foil and insulation.</u>		
Roof coverings laid to 2 degree pitch	1650sq. ft	
Roof coverings laid to 7 degree pitch	1790sq.ft	
Roof coverings laid to 10 degree pitch	1020sq.ft	
Perimeter fascia detail	1670 ft	

Perimeter fascia detail with box gutter 12" x 6" deep	3500 ft
12" x 18" deep box gutter	2600 ft
Extra for end	6 No
Rainwater hopper	3 No
Rainwater pipe 4"	690 ft
Velux Integra Solar Powered Rooflight size 4' x 6' Reference GGU 007030, laminated glass, toughened outer pane	4 No
Total	

Structural Engineer.

There are varying opinions around whether or not you should employ a structural engineer to design all of the structure to ensure all proposed work complies with building regulations. If you do employ an engineer and construct in accordance with the approved design and something goes wrong, then you will be able to rely on the engineers' and designers' insurance. If you do not construct in strict accordance with the design, you may lose the right to insurance protection.

Often, structural design is carpenter/contractor led, where he schedules say, the timber frame sizes through 'experience of what works'. It can be that his experience will get the job done and be sufficient for the expected life of the building or it may not. Will you have his insurance to rely upon going forward should structural issues arise?

There is of course, as mentioned below, the issue of over designing 'just to be sure'.

I think the important point is that you understand what you are instructing and what you are accepting. As long as you do this and are comfortable with the acknowledged risks then you should make that decision in light of all the facts.

Over-Designing.

You will soon hear talk of structural engineers 'over designing' structures. This is a universal theme of conversations among construction professionals and clients. Every client in the world is convinced the project engineer is a doom monger who always sees the worst in any structure. Even in a disaster of Armageddon proportions, the structure and the selected materials are so large and strong that your building would survive!

The owner-builder client is actually pleased to have a strong and robust building... it's the cost of the structure (no one can see or cares about) which irritates them. They want walls and stairs with slender appearances... and they get chunky! They want slim, reasonably priced steel columns... and they get large, heavy, expensive steel columns.

Luckily, at engineering school, the student structural engineers are taught to be cheery and treat all naysayers as fools who do not understand the importance of structural performance. They ask in amazement why you do not realize the wisdom of their design choices. They go on to predict terrible events occurring if a minimal reduction is sought!

All designers confidentially tell you they have come across this talk but they can recommend the one engineer in a million who does not suffer from the affliction of 'over design'. I have yet to meet an owner-builder who agrees.

Example: Engineering Calculation

Beam: FLAT ROOF JOISTS					Span: 2.8 m.	
Load name	Loading w1	Start x1	Loading w2	End x2	R1comp	R2comp
U T FLAT ROOF	1.5*0.4	0		L	0.84	0.84
					0.84	0.84
					Total load:	1.68 kN
Load types: U:UDL T: Total (positions in m. from R1)						
Maximum B.M. = 0.588 kNm at 1.40 m. from R1 Maximum S.F. = 0.840 kN at R1						
Total deflection = 0.480×10^8/EI at 1.40 m. from R1 *(E in N/mm², I in cm⁴)*						
Timber beam calculation to BS5268 Part 2: 2002 using C24 timber						
Use 47 x 147 C24 *2.9 kg/m approx*						
z = 169.3 cm³ I = 1,244 cm⁴						
Timber grade: C24 Load sharing system: K_8 = 1.1						
K_3 (loading duration factor) = 1.00 K_7 (depth factor) = 1.082 K_8 (load sharing factor) = 1.1						

> **Bending**
> Permissible bending stress, o_{rn},adrn = orn_9.K3 .K7.K8 = 7.5 x 1.00 x 1.082 x 1.1 = 8.92 N/mm^2
> Applied bending stress, o_{rn} a = 0.588 x 1000/169.3 = 3.47 N/mm^2 OK
> **Shear**
> Permissible shear stress, "adrn/l= "$_{9,11}$.K$_3$.K$_8$ = 0.71 x 1.00 x 1.1 = 0.78 N/mm^2
> Applied shear stress, "a = 0.840 x 1000 x 3/2 x 47 x 147 = 0.18 N/mm^2 OK
> **Deflection**
> Bending deflection = 0.480 x 10^8/10,800 x 1,244 = 3.57 mm
> Mid-span shear deflection = 1.2 x 0.588 x 10^6/((E/16) x 47 x 147) = 0.15 mm
> Total deflection = 3.57 + 0.15 = 3.72 mm (0.0013 L) < = 0.003L OK
>
> It is difficult to dispute matters of design with engineers as the calculations are almost undecipherable to the uninitiated. A good working relationship is the way forward.

Do you need as much steel or percentage of cement in concrete mixes as they say? Cambridge University carried out a study and their analysis concluded that, on average, designed structural beams were taking weights which were only half of their capacity. They found that carbon emissions from the manufacturing process could be cut by 11% if the steel component was decreased by 20% and the cement element of the concrete by 32%. The Canadian Society for Civil Engineering supports this by calling for designs that focus on the conservation of energy and materials.

This would be a win/win, as fewer materials reduce both the cost of the building and related carbon emissions, resulting in reduced environmental impacts. The only ones missing out would be the engineers, who like to design in ways that preclude any possibility of their insurance companies being asked to make a payment.

There will be other professional consultants you work with, but they will be job specific or site specific. The four (planner, designer, engineer and CE) will advise what you need to do and when you need other consultants.

All proposed work by all the consultants must comply with building regulations. All consultants must work together to produce an overall scheme.

TRUE STORY

> I had a difficult situation with a building budget. The windows were going to be $100,000 above projected costs on a very large home, which was adjacent to a wooded valley. After discussion with the window manufacturers, the issue became apparent. The specification called for a high level of fire rating, which was expensive to meet.

> I spoke to the designer, who had received the fire rating from the fire officer as part of the initial building inspector's process. I asked if we could reduce the specification. This was not allowed as we needed to meet the fire rating to receive a certificate of occupancy. I next spoke to the planner, who said he could not appeal as the planning permit required, we comply with the rating, though it did not specify the rating. Both the designer and the planner were adamant that a fire rating had never in their experience been reduced and we would need to accept the situation.
>
> I then contacted the fire officer, who was quite defensive as to why he had issued the rating level. In our open discussion, I assured him I was not complaining but simply wanted to understand the process. As he explained that he was asked to 'rate the lot' and the rating level was what he considered appropriate, the penny dropped. I asked if he had rated the lot or the proposed house on the lot?
>
> 'Why the lot of course, as asked', he replied.
>
> I requested if, for a further fee, he could undertake to rate the house as positioned on the lot as opposed to the greenfield lot. The rating came back with a severe fire rating on one elevation only, and a cost saving of $75,000!
>
> The officer had done as he was asked, but when asked a different and more relevant question, I received a different and more relevant response. I had not appealed the fire rating or caused a fuss; I had simply had the correct appraisal carried out.

Tradespeople.

One other group offer advice: the tradespeople who work on your project. This is usually through discussion of their work and sometimes in general conversation about how the finish on your project can be improved.

Tradespeople gain experience across many sites and a good one will see many different ways to do the same thing! It can be valuable listening to their views and learning how things may be achieved in easier ways. But in the end, you alone take responsibility.

How to source a good tradesperson;

- Recommendation is a very successful way of finding people, particularly if they are put forward by other tradespeople already doing a good job. Good tradespeople like to share a space with other good trades, as this helps them. This makes them a valuable asset when it comes to who to contact.
- Are they a member of a recognized Trade Association? This can show commitment to self-improvement, as members often attend talks on latest products and improved methods, etc.
- Do they have current public liability insurance and can they forward a copy?
- Can they provide quotations from a fixed address?
- Are they registered to pay tax, like GST, state sales tax?
- Do they have a website? Some good tradesmen do not want a web presence as they feel they are already busy enough, but specialist companies should by now be on board.
- They tend to have a good idea of their work commitments – how long in advance are they booked up for?
- Be wary of those seeking up-front funding unless you can completely understand why. It may be relevant to the placement of specialist equipment but even then, be careful. (See *A Good Deal: Book 2*)

Package Builders.

Package build companies offer an alternative solution: a complete package of work, from conceptual design to actual construction. The extent of their involvement varies greatly. It can be the whole house completely finished on their land or yours. Or they shall work from your prepared foundations and structural slab, use your drains and simply construct the shell and external features. This includes items such as roofs, windows, internal floors and stairs. There are many different approaches and offered solutions.

The advantage of using the package companies is clarity of costs. They may not be as economical as you putting every element together yourself, but they offer assurances. They work within their 'house style' and standards, so you can be confident over design and quality.

Project Milestones

It can be useful to draw up a programme of intended milestones. This confirms you considered and included the professional team and contractors agreed milestone dates for the project to be delivered.

It's time to fill out your milestone chart in a spreadsheet. Consider your professional team and question how long they want to reach a given or fixed achievement. List these dates as your set target dates. Part of the process is also holding yourself to account. So, list the dates that you instruct your professional advisors. How well will you fare?

What can be eye-opening is an 'achievement' column, which records the number of days of delay. No column is included for the number of days that you are in advance, as this just doesn't happen, but the chart can be adjusted to suit your individual circumstances.

As the delays build up and escalate, the total delay can be distressing and alarming for you. Holiday periods come and go, as do public holidays, which all add to the total delay. Nonetheless, the purpose of the milestone chart is to highlight where the delays are and encourage you to quickly react and reduce their impact. It also galvanizes the resolve of your team to know that dates and deadlines are taken seriously. When they give you an undertaking, you expect it to be met.

Project Milestone Dates

Milestone	Planned	Actual	Item Delay
Appoint Planner	1-Feb	5-Feb	5 Days
Appoint Designer	1-Feb	5-Feb	5 Days
Appoint Engineer	5-Feb	12-Feb	8 Days
Appoint Land Survey	10-Feb	1-Mar	20 Days
Appoint Hydrological Engineer	10-Feb	7-Mar	26 Days
Appoint CE (PQS)	10-Feb	17-Mar	36 Days
Professional Team Appointed	10-Feb	17-Mar	35 Days
Land Survey	15-Feb	1-Apr	60 days
Hydrology Report	15-Feb	12-Apr	57 Days
Planning Reports Prepared	15-Mar	1-May	62 Days
Concept Design for Discussion - Stage 1	1-Apr	15-Jun	76 Days
Pre-Application Planning	8-May	1-Aug	86 Days
Prepare Scheme	1-Jun	1-Sep	93 Days
Freeze Scheme - Stage 2	10-Jun	1-Oct	114 Days
Submit Planning Application	12-Jun	3-Oct	114 Days
Planning Decision	15-Aug	15-Jan	154 Days
	Planned	196 Days	
	Delay	154 Days	
	Total	349 Days	
• Chart emphasizes how delays cascade.			
• First date & end date included in calculation.			
• No column provided for time ahead of schedule.			

Consultant Procurement Schedule.

A private document that is well worthwhile preparing is a schedule of consultant procurement. As part of your initial costs, you should identify a *group cost* for your consultant's.

By listing your consultants individually on a spreadsheet and filling in relevant information, you can visually track what their proposals are and what costs you are running up. This can help you decide on the selection of your team and the value they bring to your project.

Chapter 6 – Action

- Get organized!
- Check everyone's insurances
- Talk to your consultants – pick their brains
- Prepare a milestone/consultants chart
- Talk to your tradespeople
- Look at what package builders offer
- Commence consultant team selection

LEGAL
Purchase Occurs
Insurance in place

TIME
Milestones chart
Outline works programme

MONEY
Calculate wealth
Prepare budget costs

DESIGN
Work through with design team
Confirm planning status and take action
Name check consultants
Soil inspection
Site Survey

GENERAL
Identify infrastructure companies

CHAPTER 7
SUMMARY

A program is produced to marshal thoughts and allow the designer to produce a building reflecting the owner-builder's tastes.

Highlights covered in this chapter include:

- Preliminary planning and space layouts
- Neutral Reach Zone
- Creating the first draft
- Lifetime Home considerations
- Value Engineering
- Buildability
- Sustainability
- Permit reports
- Permit refusals are not allowed to happen

CHAPTER 7

DESIGNER'S PROGRAM & PERMIT APPLICATION

'Design adds value faster than it adds costs'.
– Joel Spolsky

The 'designers program' is literally named: it is a program where you agree with your designer what it is you want from the project. Defining your needs, even in outline form, gives the designer a starting point to develop the plans. It is helpful if you have an idea of what type of *look* you want. Seek out examples of the designer's previous work to reassure yourself and your family that you like their style and approach. Or perhaps you feel they are the right people to design a building to meet local architectural characteristics. Everything needs a starting point, and this is yours.

New home builders instructing designers are often a little wary of what to say and how much input to offer. This is understandable, as one does not want to show complete ignorance or be a 'smart aleck' who knows it all but is then shown to know very little.

Designers prefer that you list and describe your requirements, not to present them with drawings of your solution. Your written program may spark solutions different from those you visualized, some of which might just be clever and acceptable.

Just be yourself as you help the designer build up a picture of you and your family and the purpose of your new home.

- Is it intended to be a statement piece or just a shelter?
- Is it an environmental message of what can be aspired to?
- Are you following an existing lifestyle choice?
- Or do you just want somewhere clean and modern?

The program is certainly not a single opportunity document to encapsulate all the input needed to design your future home. The program is far from the final document. It draws out your requirements and melds this with visions of how well things can be done. Think of it as a document the whole family can contribute to; what do they want and how can they help?

Changes will occur, budgets updated, initially brilliant ideas may eventually seem less brilliant and unexpected decisions will be made. The function of the home must be addressed, as will the style (or look). All are important and all must be given due regard. The design will emerge in time; rarely does the perfect answer appear without in-depth design changes. What seemed obvious as 'standard' at the beginning is improved, changed and modified. This process of change sharpens and improves the end product – the quality of your home.

Producing the Program

Checklists are often generated by the design consultants to ensure all the relevant information is captured. Through conversation they coax out of you and your partner what you want and what you need. Is what you both want the same or are there differences of approach?

Your designer will soon request a *site survey* is carried out. A professional surveyor will produce an accurate digital survey showing the boundaries and levels across the site. This is used to produce a measured site drawing that can be relied upon.

Most designers will only produce sketches after they receive a digital survey and use this as their starting point.

The designer will produce space layouts to show relationships of spaces to each other. These space layouts, when visualized with a specific lot of land, produce clarity of thought. This initial clarity may be a long way from the completed project design, but it will certainly be a good place to commence the design process.

Preliminary Planning.

The designer will often start with a bubble diagram. This will create a not-to-scale and not-dimensioned illustration. It is the designer's attempt to visually describe what they are hearing. You may not feel it represents what you are saying, and your honest response is the whole point.

The bubbles will initially be positioned next to each other producing a flow. Perhaps all the bedrooms close by at one end of the diagram or put teenage or guest rooms at the furthest point. The rear yard will be off the main living areas or kitchen. They will show relationships, not fixed designs. Each bubble will be named by a description of its use. For example, ensuite bathroom as opposed to main bathroom.

The designer will continue this thought pattern through to the next stage and produce a room/area sketch. This will show relative sizes for each named area and show what is next to each other and overall relationships of the spaces.

The conceptual process continues and drawings are created, showing sizes and positions of spaces and also indicating the floor area of the home.

The designer then produces a scheme they feel meets your program.

Be super critical (silently) and go over each and every point. Improvements are made by dedicated scrutiny. This is not to infer the designer has not presented something very suitable, it is simply that you want it to be the best it can be. One little change leads to other thoughts and the design sharpens and gets 'tighter'. It is far, far easier to critique something than create something.

Basic building codes will be added to the mix. Room sizes will be above the minimum, as dictated by the building codes, and the overall external heights are restricted to those likely demanded by the planners. Staircases will be set at acceptable widths and pitches, with landings sized for comfortable furniture movement.

How well the footprint of the house is situated on the site will be looked at and space allocated for living rooms and sleeping and wet room areas (such as kitchen, bathrooms and laundry facilities). Window sizes and orientation will be suggested to take into account sunrises and sunsets and the overall street frontage of the property. How will you move around the home and what spaces interact with each other?

You should consider both what works in your current home and what you would like to develop and change. What benefits not currently met, will the new home bring?

Start collecting images you admire from magazines or from websites that you think are worth exploring. Try to show the designer where your taste lies. Be encouraged to collaborate to get the feel and finish you want. This can be described as aiding sharpness of design or blending of materials. All are valid and are all worth discussing.

Sometimes an idea mentioned can become pivotal; a feature that sets the whole tone. All designers can recall how a single feature mentioned early on became the defining feature of the home.

> **TRUE STORY**
>
> We were once looking at a lot with great sea views. We wanted to tip our hat to the nautical feel but to keep away from portholes and the like. Through discussion, someone mentioned a pier, and the whole house design fell into place. The house was laid out in two parts: a living side and a sleeping side. Both were divided by a central 'pier' running from the rear yard through to the front external area. The team had fun making it look like a pier. And so the dramatic and modern 'Pier House' was built.

Consider what moved you to purchase this particular lot. Are there special features you particularly like that are important to maintain?

Also consider the wider possibilities. Outdoor areas can be designed to give you a feeling of a special private place. Front areas of the property can be opened up to promote vision and safety. All areas are to be balanced and due consideration given.

Do you work from home? What is your lifestyle? What about life stages; do you wish to include separate areas for granny or older teenagers? How much storage can you squeeze in, as opposed to how much has been allowed?

Timing is a difficult subject. Often the pre-permit, preparation stage takes as long or longer than the build stage. Just how long it takes to get the project from program to completion is best judged more than calculated. Time blocks can be allocated for each stage, but many of the timings are out of your hands. Instead, they are driven by others who play a part in approving and issuing permits.

Then there is the matter of *your* time commitment and what type of owner-builder you will be. *Hands on* and on-site day and night is completely different to the detached visiting manager who takes on an overseeing role.

The issue of budgets will be raised by your designer and these are difficult to assess. I mean, you have not yet got a design let alone a detailed cost analysis. A budget will nonetheless need to be presented, so that scope and size can be developed.

Try to crystallize your specific reasons for wanting to build your own home. This becomes the starting point for preferences. You can then assess your options and commence the decision-making phase.

You will continue to make decisions throughout the process, but the first key choices will set the major features of the home and set the character of the completed project.

Firming Up the Designer's Program.

The designer will produce a conceptual outline of a structure. Just check that you are all on the same page going forward. This confirmation will lead to floor plans and layouts positioning the bedrooms and living areas. Things can still markedly change, but you'll have a flavour of where the process is going.

Site orientation will be the first concern. What direction will the building face? This is usually an obvious choice, with the entrance located in a convenient and logical position. The survey will allow your designer to accurately fix the position of the house, along with considering issues such as overlooking from your neighbors or vice versa, rights of light and consideration of views.

By now, you will be actively thinking through the style of the proposed home; yet it is only after you focus on the designs as a project that the pieces fit together. You should ask your designer for a plan of the proposed house, with dimensions to show sizes, external elevations, floor area and external wall distances from adjacent boundaries. The discussion starts in earnest over the size and material choices for the property.

The scope of the work will be indicated on the drawings. Notes state materials to be used and standards or regulations to be met. A cross-section of the house may indicate the type of foundation, with other drawings showing selected layouts, total sizes of the rooms, external elevations, roof and window details, etc.

The scope document will also show the layout and flow of the house. Is it over a single storey? How do areas of the home interconnect with each other? Will common areas such as family rooms be adjacent to the kitchen or laundry rooms? This sets the feel of the living spaces. It will show the floor area of each room and the total floor area as proposed.

Consider the different areas as *uses* as opposed to spaces. How do you intend to use the house? Imagine yourself living there. Some areas are best connected to each other and some are best left separate. An example is the kitchen, which is best next to the dining area, and the noise-producing living areas, which are best distant from bedrooms. Overall, this is a defining document and a form is taking shape.

The challenge is to deliver the home project envisaged within time and budget. Remember, your consultants will help you ensure all the items of work are included. You are striving for clarity on what work you will do yourself and what work contractors are employed to carry out. A clear scope helps clear thinking by all the players.

Windows and doors can be tweaked to take advantage of views and the sun's position at different times of the year. The roofs should be considered as places to fit solar panels, while space may be allocated within the premises to store electrical batteries now or in the future.

What type of heating is to be installed?

Natural gas or electricity, air or underground heat pumps: they all have different layout requirements.

Are external balconies wanted?

Or, are you looking to construct with flat wall surfaces on the exterior?

Is the house secure from intruders?

Can you grow old in this house?

Is it adaptable to you ageing and requiring better access to a split-level design or upper floors? These points and many others are all things to consider.

Terms to be included in the conversation are 'energy efficiency', 'low maintenance' 'sustainability' and 'quality of work and finish'. Other points, such as room sizes and discussions of how each room is used, are all decisions taken after considering the orientation of the site. Many other issues will arise, from the structure to services and finishes, and these should all be dealt with in a logical manner.

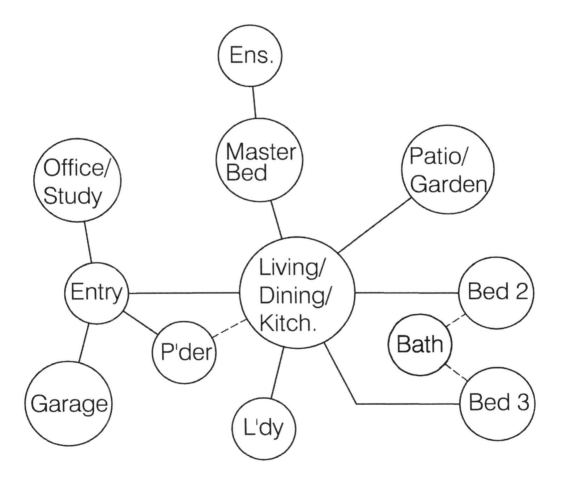

PHILIP FITZPATRICK

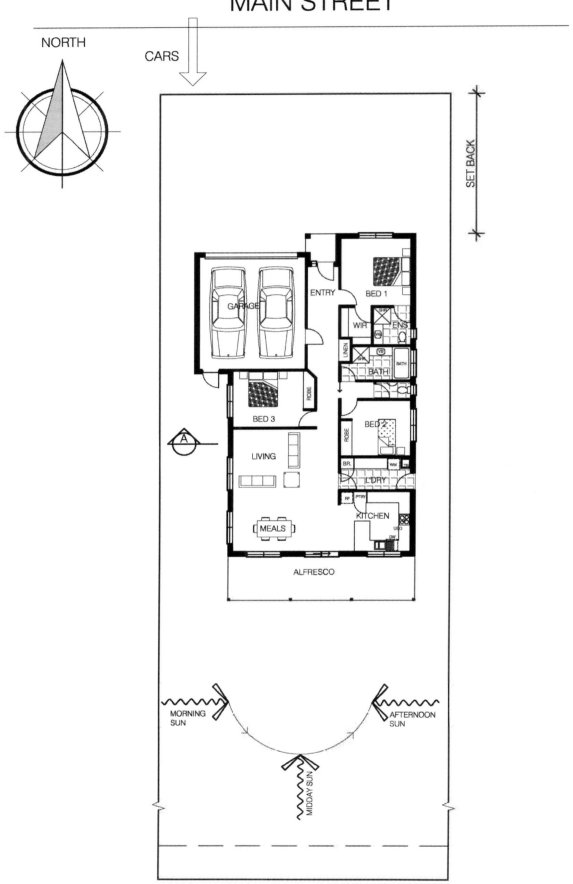

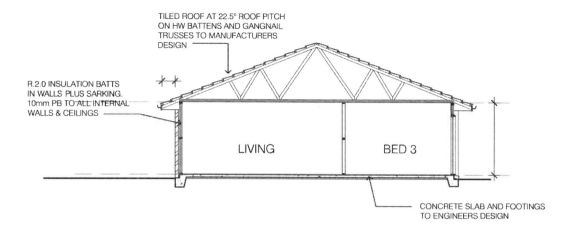

TYPICAL SECTION THROUGH

The designer will seldom also be a structural engineer and so the question of the structure will arise as an early decision. The designer will have opinions on local suitability and best practice. You should discuss common options for foundation and types of structural walls. It is important you understand the basic choices available. In the end, the structure has to be cost effective and be in place to support the house.

Engineer/Geotechnical Survey.

You will not usually at this stage need a full structural design, although it is common to get *outline advice* from a structural engineer. This will ensure you are on the right track. This also ensures you'll have a professional opinion on your proposals.

While the above is generally true, this is all dependent on your local planning requirements. You may need to submit structural information as part of your building permit application. This is particularly the case if you are constructing a basement. With such a proposal, you will need the services of a structural engineer.

Your engineer will likely suggest a geotechnical survey is carried out. For this a specialist consultant is instructed, who will visit site to drill an auger into the earth and take soil samples. These will be tested in an offsite laboratory to determine the sub-ground make-up, the soil strength, composition, water content, and other important characteristics. Their report will provide the engineer with valuable information to assist the foundation design.

Principles.

The principles are simple. It's the maths and the allowances the structural engineer must include in any given situation that are difficult! The engineer will also allow for wind loads and possible external earth conditions. All (reasonably possible) conditions must be accounted for. This is why engineering allowances made in any given condition are unique to your property and are based on your location and ground conditions.

The Foundation is the base that all weights from the building will eventually settle on and transfer into the soil.

The foundation must take 'dead loads' and 'live loads'.

Dead Loads are the weight of the structure, roof, windows, etc. These do not change once construction is complete.

Live Loads are the weights added once the building becomes occupied. This can be furniture, people, snow etc. These are a mixture of fixed and moving loads. For example, sports stadia can have thousands of people jumping up and down while storage facilities have static stored goods; both are examples of live loads.

Structural systems fall into two main categories:

- Load bearing walls, with openings that support walls above by way of lintels or arches.
- Frameworks of columns and beams. These are commonly constructed of timber, steel or reinforced concrete.

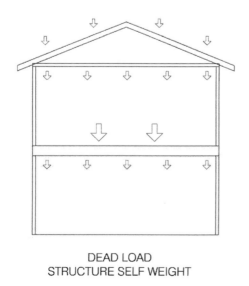

DEAD LOAD
STRUCTURE SELF WEIGHT

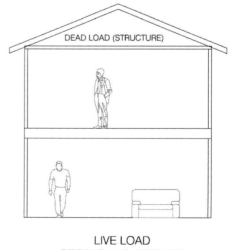

LIVE LOAD
PEOPLE AND FITTINGS

Basements.

Basements are increasing in popularity almost everywhere outside of North America, where they have been popular for decades.

Keeping dry is the number one issue for a basement. A damp basement is a nightmare, as dampness is not the friend of equipment or stored goods. Painstaking detailing of the construction process and careful installation is the only way to avoid dampness. By earth pressing up against the external walls, hydrostatic pressures are introduced, which encourages water to find even the smallest of gaps to infiltrate. A waterproof barrier known as a 'waterproofing membrane' is installed to stop moisture entering through the structure.

Be aware of any penetrations through the basement structure. Try to route drains and services in such a way that penetrations to the membranes are at a minimum, as a break in the membrane is a weak spot. Check against even the smallest damage to the *waterproofing membranes* and carry out repairs before the membrane is covered by the wall or floor structure.

The engineer needs to design a sufficient structure and the designer, along with your specialist damp-proofing contractor, need to agree on a fool-proof plan to stop water from entering.

Only employ a specialist damp-proofing contractor who can offer an insurance-backed guarantee. Then if the contractor retires or ceases trading, the insurance policy is in place.

Q. What could possibly go wrong?
A. Everything. You must evaluate the design and consider what it takes to design out damp.

The design of many damp-proof schemes do not stop water from entering. The system relies on a vertical, impervious membrane that diverts the water before it has entered the structure. These schemes may rely on a sump and pump system. If this is suggested: first investigate gravity as the way of diverting the water. Mechanical pumps will eventually let you down, but gravity never will.

If you must have a pump, make sure it is a double pump, with a spare motor to operate automatically when the first fails. An alarm system is a must too, as it will alert you when the first pump fails.

> **TRUE STORY.**
>
> The English medieval cathedral, York Minster, suffered a terrible fire in 1984. The firefighters forced hose pipes of pressured water into the church and the water jet pressure pulled down the burning roof. The fire department was concerned the rising water would also cause damage to the building and the invaluable artefacts. They knew the pumps could not pump water out at anything like the pace the hoses could bring water in.
>
> Under the grates on the church floor was an unseen ally. A drain installed by the Romans some 1,900 years earlier was full of silt *but still functioning*. Gravity had not gone out of fashion and the clay pipe still did its job.
>
> The water drained away at speed and the artefacts were saved.
>
> You never hear a story of a Roman mechanical pump still working two millennia later!

The designer will produce a series of drawings based on the survey plan to illustrate:

- Site Plan
- Floor Plans
- Roof Plan
- Drainage Plan
- Sections and Elevations
- Construction details
- Window/Door/Sanitary schedules

Neutral Reach Zones (NRZ).

Anthropometry is the study of humans, including what size and proportion is average for say a person in a Western society or in an Asian society. Ergonomics is the science behind the size and design of objects to make them appropriate for human use. Industrial Designers take all this information and feed it into the products manufactured. It also informs the height and location of where things are placed.

An efficient point to place something is called the 'Neutral Reach Zone'. For example, items on a kitchen work surface are ideally in this zone, so that the vast majority of people can easily access and use the equipment. By having things conveniently placed, the possibility of injury or muscle strain is reduced... and it just makes life a lot easier!

Ergonomics and User Needs.

The rise of a staircase or the height of a door handle are common examples of ergonomics working in your world. They are set at heights to match most users' body sizes and yet not unusable for people at the *end-ish* part of normal as far as size is concerned.

If one of the users is a person with disability or a wheelchair user, then take care to design to also meet their needs. Modifications to allow access could include a section of the worktop in the kitchen put lower than the other areas, or corridors and doors made wider than usual.

It's important for you to consider what you need to design into the home. This is to personalise the house so you can live there as easily as possible. The designer will assist, but it will enhance the design if you can put forward all special (or not even that special) requirements.

When you are walking around other people's homes, identify the zones and see how well the building has been designed. Notice when things work well from your perspective, and more importantly, when things do not. Look at kitchens and the spaces around food preparation and the relative positions of the refrigerator, kitchen sink and oven.

These observations will feed into the house design, as it sets off a train of thought in areas where you perform certain tasks, such as cooking or laundry. Consider working spaces and distances between rooms and zones.

Kitchens are often considered best positioned in the center of the home, where direct access is available in many directions and from where children can be observed and supervised.

Stairs are regulated and must be constructed within certain parameters. You should consider the number of steps in a flight until you reach a landing, the size of the landing, the pitch of the stair flight, the height of handrail (if it is on one side only or both sides) and overall, how accessible the design is for you today and in the future.

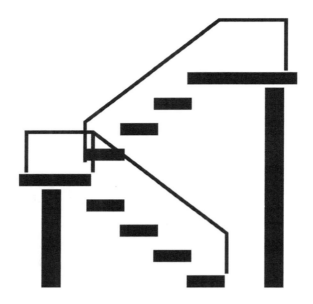

Buildability/Constructability.

Buildability (Constructability) should be continuously considered, alongside sustainability, maintenance and access. The theory is, if you can construct efficiently with designs that include consideration of the actual construction process, then the build will be easier, efficient and cheaper.

Designers are still educated separately from constructors; in fact, architects, surveyors and engineers are all educated apart and are not linked to the people who do the installation work in any way as any part of their training.

The designer, as second nature, will still make many of these construction decisions. For example, they will normally show door openings at standard manufactured door sizes. This means, for example, doors can be purchased more economically as the manufacturer will charge more for a one-off special design.

That doesn't mean you're constrained to standard. If you want to make an architectural statement with a special sized door, then this can be allowed within the scheme. Cost and allowances will be made accordingly. This theory is taken across all elements of the build, including room sizes. Therefore, materials waste can be reduced on, say, cutting tiles, since the room has been designed with a particular sized tile in mind.

The level of on-site build accuracy can be daunting, but it does lead into considering what can be manufactured off-site and brought to site complete. Are you better off installing a few larger items than lots of smaller items? Modern Methods of

Construction (MMC) spring from offsite manufacture and larger completed or semi-completed installations.

Many manufacturers supply items pre-made, such as doors, windows, shower trays, basins and vanity units, whole bath pods, and the common kitchen unit. All are made to standard sizes and so the rooms can be sized to accommodate them. This makes the build cheaper and more straightforward. The benefit also comes by you (the build supervisor) seeing the unit fit snugly into the designed space and you not having to check around for the closest one to fit, even if undersized. If down the line you wish to replace a unit, a standard size will be more readily available than a specially designed item.

Finished products, such as locks, door furniture, light fittings, power points, covings, etc. are also made to standard designs and sizes, and in some ways, your internal design is simply putting these products together to give you the finished look. The earlier you select the finish and type, the more well-fitting the house will be.

Sustainability.

Sustainability has become a mainstream feature of design. House building has a major role to play in protecting natural resources and your selections play a part. In this modern world we consume at ever faster rates so we should encourage the use of renewable resources wherever possible.

Consider options that enhance rather than detract. Planting outdoor areas can reduce pollutants coming into the home, while green foliage on the external walls or shading with landscaping can reduce internal temperatures. Natural materials can be used for insulation. Birds and wildlife benefit from green sedum roofs.

Across the construction industry, many professionals are proud to include sustainable materials with a low carbon impact. Green building technologies are now available in all construction products and materials. The benefits of low energy use in the manufacturing process and to the house occupier have become self-evident.

Similarly, there is no reason the owner/builder cannot build their house to the highest green standards they can. Investigate the latest offerings from wind power, photovoltaic (PV) solar panels and battery storage, ground source and air heat pumps, but do not forget how much energy is lost through windows, doors and poor insulation.

Seek out sustainability schemes you can join and list items of positive action you can benchmark your build against. Check how green your proposed build is – with online assessment tools.

Cold (Thermal) Bridging.

Cold Bridging is both damaging and avoidable. I'll explain. Significant heat loss occurs through gaps in the building insulation. These gaps create a route for colder external temperatures to suck out heat you have paid to generate and you will pay to replace. Condensation can occur and dampness, along with mold growth, can result. By designing with thought and providing a continuous barrier at junctions of walls, floors and roofs, cold bridging can be avoided.

Passive House.

Passive House buildings use little energy and provide a high quality of air and comfort. The basics of a good passive house design are covered by the following:

- Plan your solar design to keep heat or shield heat within the structure as appropriate
- Take care over openings for high quality windows and doors
- Install an efficient mechanical air ventilation recovery system
- Be careful with design detailing to avoid cold bridging
- An airtight home is crucial
- Think through material selection, for example timber studs in external walls are far more thermally effective than steel studs

As with almost every point in the home development, deciding to build a highly insulated passive home is best designed from the start. It is never as good as a retrospective decision.

Your designers should select the structural frame with this intention in mind and good decisions will follow.

The Passive House Institute produce their Passive House Planning Package (PHPP) – software to assist you to meet their design criteria and recommendations. Certification is available for your home if you register and follow their exacting standards. They claim their Passive House concept is the 'the only internationally recognized, performance-based energy standard in construction'. As leaders in energy performance, they are at the forefront of energy efficient construction technologies. The Passive House Institute US inc. (PHIUS) promote this, as do Passive House Canada, and both are a good source of information.

Lifetime Home Standards.

Lifetime Home Standards are where you consider what awaits you in the future. We are all getting older and our needs change quickly, with reduced mobility sometimes coming on faster than we hope. Most people like to remain in their own homes as long as they can.

By having considered and built in flexible designs at the time of home construction, you increase the chances of remaining longer and more comfortably in your home. Changes can then be simply made at a future point. An example of considered design is widening the doorway to a bathroom, in case wheelchair access is needed down the track.

Again, it's not only what you put in, but what you leave as space for the future which can make a difference. You can design the home so a simple rearrangement will allow the living areas to be transformed onto a single level, if this becomes necessary.

Space for a future elevator can also be accommodated within the design. Taking this further, the floor structure can be trimmed so that structurally a new installation can be 'punched' through without major works. In the spirit of future-proofing, an electrical service run to an adjacent point can prove to be a wise decision, retrospectively.

Observing.

If you can note some local homes you admire, and even better, describe why you like them, it can give you something to aim for and assist your designer in the design approach. An image of a room or feature or a style of home you liked can be used as a starting point. This is the time to bring it up. Everything goes into this discussion. It can be something as simple as a fence or railing you have spotted, and by taking an image, you can show the type of feature you like.

This part of the process is the most pleasant. You are having fun imagining the joy you will have in your new home, and all is well with the world. Envisioning can also be brought to life, because designers often produce computer generated images (CGIs) illustrating internal areas and external images. These will show colors and 3D views of how well the house will serve your needs.

Performance Gap.

Research has revealed a large difference between how much energy is *used* in a functioning building compared to how much energy was *predicted* during the planning process. In some cases, five times as much energy was recorded as needed to keep the property running. This can be an unpleasant reality check.

This difference is called the 'performance gap'. On completion, performance checks by way of air leakage tests and infrared photographic imaging can show in stark detail how well or how poorly the building envelope has been insulated and sealed. Careful detailing and installation during the construction process has a huge impact on how well the building performs.

It is becoming more common for planning permits for apartment buildings to state that the construction works and the completed scheme must meet *neutral air quality* benchmarks. This could move onto individual homes in certain areas of higher air pollution. The idea is that your building does not add pollutants to the atmosphere. These pollutants mainly come from boilers and traffic. To meet these requirements, you may need to design in high levels of insulation to reduce fossil fuel use and select environmentally friendly heating equipment. They will also like you to prioritise sustainable modes of transport.

You may be required to install monitoring equipment and the local municipality may impose a financial penalty if the standards are not met. If you go to the trouble of detailing carefully and installing monitoring equipment, only to find your external building fabric was not installed correctly, it can be a source of distress for you. You also pay unnecessary amounts for fuel, and if the local authority levies an increased tax, as part of their 'green agenda', you also have to pay for this.

This is a lose/lose situation which can be avoided by you effectively managing the build process. All operatives and contractors should be warned you are planning an air-test of the building on completion. This will confirm how good they were!

Performance.

The Standard Assessment Process (SAP) calculations indicate how well the building environmentally performs on completion. By checking and monitoring over a 12-month period, you can determine how well it has been done… and see if you are living the dream or living in a fool's paradise.

In summary, the days of not acting on climate change are over and you must accept real action will need to be taken and local municipalities will impose stringent requirements.

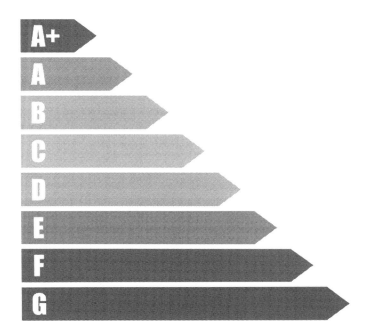

Evaluation of the Scheme.

Once the design team have sent you what they consider to be a good proposal, you should feel excited and believe that the layouts and elevations are very much in line with a home you would love to live in. If nagging doubts exist, this is the moment to raise them. After this point you should move forward and submit this concept to the planners for approval.

Just before you 'fix and freeze' the scheme, it can be worthwhile to take stock and review the decisions made.

Practicalities of Living in the Home.

Look at the windows and see how they will be opened and closed. Are the handles too high for you or an average person to reach? If this is the case, consider amending the design or introducing electrically powered, remote controlled window-openers. I use this example because if you cannot safely open a window to allow fresh air in and stale air to escape, then a large part of the function of the window is lost.

This exercise can be extended in each area of the building. How do you access a loft area? Can all the kitchen cupboards be reached? This process can be extended to ease of access as well. Are power points placed conveniently?

> **TIP BOX**
>
> What is Value Engineering?
>
> **Value Engineering** is a conscious and explicit set of disciplined procedures designed to seek out optimum **value** for both initial and long-term investment.
>
> – Whole Building Design Guide (Wbdg.org)

Value Engineering (VE)

A term used in construction around the agreement of the program is *value engineering*. This means that after the design stage, the project is looked at holistically and the key decisions previously made are reviewed.

In home building, a lot of people like standard solutions. This could be the type of glazing to the window frames (say, double) or roof covering (say, tile). Standard solutions bring standard costs which are always cheaper than 'special' costs.

Questions to ask yourself:

- Are the material solutions and selections as good as they could be?
- Could the functions of the spaces be increased or improved?
- Are you getting value for money?

VE involves reviewing if the current house design's function and cost can be improved. Any improvements should seek to raise the quality of the project. Costs are improved by lowering the price on a like-for-like basis.

Designers are often reluctant to co-operate with this process in a meaningful way. This is a shame because what could be an extremely valuable tool and assist the project in 'tightening up' can be missed. Designers often say they have gone through this process already by this stage, so claim that any changes or savings will only dilute their design concept. The argument often put forward is, 'you indicated a budget and all the indications are the design meets this budget'. So, why water down a good design?

This designer is speaking as a true artist would, not unlike one who is protecting their art installation. As the owner and owner-builder, you have other loyalties as well. Loyalties to your family and concerns over the financial commitments you have to meet.

Of course, you have not even applied for a building permit, let alone got approval or commenced any work. How can you be sure at this stage if your budget will pan out?

Why Undertake a VE Exercise?

Some would say bluntly 'to save money'… or perhaps to clarify how much money is needed to complete the project.

Now the design is complete, it's sensible that all decisions taken during the process are reviewed to ensure the most appropriate material selection was achieved.

If you take all these points (saving money and improving the material selections) as your aim, you can see why the designers are opposed in principle to you re-evaluating their design. It is not the intention of value engineering to cause distress to the designer, but rather to make the house better. This is in both design and function. If the house is easier to build, is cheaper to build and yet you ensure the integrity of the design is retained, what is there not to like?

The designer may be troubled that you are not maintaining the integrity of the design and are swayed by savings, which potentially lessens their concept and design. Ownership and owner-building has challenges and this is one of them.

You must decide if you want to go through the value engineering process or if you'll go with the design proposals as currently laid out.

Large government or major landmark projects often employ a specialist team of consultants to carry out such VE reviews, with only input from the original designer. In brainstorming sessions over a set number of days, they argue within their disciplines and expertise as to what can be recommended as their contribution to the value engineering exercise.

I recommend a more modest approach, but one which can be effective. I suggest you print off a few copies of the plans and elevations and look at them in great detail. Perhaps go over them with a knowledgeable friend who has not been involved up to this point. This is done to bring a fresh view and seek outside input. You can note on the drawings any materials or finishes you would consider using.

A question to ask yourself when you are looking at each area and room is: *what does this room do?* This may seem an obvious question for, say, a bedroom, but is it?

Who will occupy the room and what activities will take place, remembering young children have different requirements to teenagers? Will the room be used for school study or music playing?

The question can be phrased as *'what does it do and what else does it do?'*

It's surprising how many spaces are multi-functional. To design this at the earliest stage is beneficial for the design and also dramatically improves the outcome of the finished product. This process goes back and forth until you are clued up on who will use each area and the whole package seems to check all the boxes.

Now is a good time to consider the type of finish you think fits your style. This is not to slavishly copy others, but to give a feeling or atmosphere and to adapt these features into the design.

Area Name	What does it do?	What else does it do?
Front Door External	Somewhere to stand to open the front door.	An area for visitors to enter your home. First impression are important.
Front Door Internal	Door mat and side table space.	Closet.
Hallway	Access to stairs and living room.	Access to ground floor WC.
Stairs	An accessway between floor levels.	A feature of the hallway.
Ground Floor WC	WC on living room level.	Wet umbrella stand.
Living Areas	Seating area.	TV and entertainment.
Family Areas	Seating adjacent to kitchen.	Children homework/play.
Kitchen Areas	Cook meals.	Dine at breakfast bar.
Dining Areas	A place for family meals.	An entertainment area of the home.
Rear External Areas	Conservatory.	Plants & coffee area.
Future Elevator Space	Provides a clear position to fit a future domestic elevator.	Allows you the flexibility to remain in your home if you are unable to climb the stairs
Laundry	Position of washing machine and dryer.	Ironing board storage & linen cupboard.
Bathrooms	Facilities for children & guests.	Add bath for children with separate shower.
En-Suite Bathrooms	A place to use WC and washing facilities.	A place of privacy.
Master Bedroom	Our bathroom.	Add extra wash hand basin.
Bedroom 2	A place for guests to sleep.	A place to offer to guests as part of their stay. Care may be taken with views/light/facilities etc.
Bedroom 3	A place for a child to sleep.	Homework/instrument practice/toy storage/how old will the child be in two years?

Once you establish an outline budget, an interesting question is: what would it mean if I budgeted either 10% more or 10% less? This can bring new perspective. What aspirations do you have? What would you like to include if things go well and natural savings are made? What should be the first casualty if things go amiss? This is all part of the flexibility you must have to deliver your project.

If you decide to go through a process of Value Engineering, the CE can be the most helpful person on the team. They are not tied up on specification excellence; moreover, they take the attitude: does it comply and will it do the same job, but cheaper?

The designer may not be best pleased by this value perspective, 'but those are the breaks'.

In fairness, a lot of designers also prepare specifications of works in much the same way as a CE. This is not, however, the middle of their expertise, while it *is* at the heart of the CE's area.

Results.

Take a 'visual walk' through the building to include easy maintenance features.

Ensure you have plenty of copies of the drawings and make notes, refining in broad terms what it is you want. Consider the materials you select and review alternatives.

Once you have a workable scheme, sit down with the people who will share your home and 'walk' through the scheme, going over each room and aspect in as much detail as you can.

Schemes always benefit from an overall review before they are fixed and firm decisions are made.

Go back to the designer and share your thoughts. The design is getting close to being right for you and your family. The purpose is to produce a 'better' home, with the room sizes, features and style you like at a budget you can afford.

Maintenance.

Maintenance of the building is also an important consideration. The house will exist for many years and easier maintenance is always good. Consider what regular jobs will need to be done to keep the home in good working order.

Examples of designing in easier maintenance are:

- Consideration of how you will access gutters and if you will include gutter protectors (aka helmets) to reduce debris build-up?
- Factoring in space around furnaces, boilers and tanks to make servicing easier.
- Properly designed access panels for water traps and pipes, to prevent damaged finishes.

The clever part is thinking ahead and planning how you can make maintenance simpler. Your designer will probably have considered this point, but it is always good to check. Some building codes require safe access for workmen. This can be expensive if you have roof mounted equipment within 78" (2.0m) of the roof edge.

Zoning Permit Process/Building Permit Process

As discussed in Chapter 2, some municipalities combine these two permits and some keep them separate. As ever you will have to follow local application procedures and practice.

When the design is getting close to 'freezing', the designer can provide layouts for a building permit submission. A designer can skillfully assist you through these initial stages.

It's important you constantly update your financial projections. As more information becomes available, you'll get a clearer view of what funds you need. Even if your design or scheme is not considered by others to be out of keeping with the area or in any way controversial, discuss with your designer if it would help to meet with the planning officer prior to submission.

In an ideal world, the planning officer will fully consider your application and make recommendations on how to improve your application and the likelihood of it having a favorable reception. In the real world, the reception you receive from planning authorities varies greatly. You will have to navigate local custom. Some charge a substantial sum for pre-application advice; some give it freely and some give none at all until after a full submission. Even if the town web site indicates that pre-application advice is not available, try to discuss your design with the municipal planning officers before officially submitting your application. Their advice can be important and save time and money.

Permit Reports.

Ask your designer which reports and documents you are likely to need to include as part of your build permit application. The reports required are dependent upon site conditions/location, previous site use, your particular design, the surrounding area/zone, and how-close-your-neighbors-are.

In some areas, basic project specifications are required as part of the building permit submission. Where this is a requirement, a specification booklet is available to be purchased to meet this need. Your designer will be able to help you fill in the non-standard responses.

Fire services, refuse services, traffic control authorities, police, etc. are also commonly asked to comment on planning and design proposals, and their response is often required before a decision can be made.

Your designer or planning consultant will advise you if any supplementary information is required as part of the planning process. Sometimes items or reports arise as additional requests for clarification during the process and sometimes they are needed regardless of the application. These can cover many items of building safety and how the scheme has a bearing on surrounding properties or the local areas.

Some planning authorities defer responsibility from themselves by asking for expert reports from outside consultants (such as engineers). Through this process, they can show they have comprehensively considered all the implications of your application… even though it is suspected that they already know the answer.

A great example of this is flood assessment reports. Some authorities ask for a site-specific report for each scheme in their area. The reports come back with the same response as the one they previously received for an application around the corner. But they can claim thoroughness at your expense.

These reports can be required for many reasons, for example, to meet environmental concerns, energy efficiency, basement impact studies, potential loss of light to adjacent properties, noise levels from traffic, effect of your construction plan on substantial trees and so on. You must address all of these points methodically and respond formally to their concerns. If not, you will not meet the planner's required information requests. You will likely be refused a building permit or the decision on your application will be postponed until you comply.

The builder or in this case you, as the Owner-Builder will usually submit the building permit application. Many professional builders have worked in their areas for many years and have developed good working relationships with the staff at the local offices, so they likely know what the primary areas of concern (or 'hot button' issues) will be. Discuss your approach for all aspects of the permitting application process with your design team to make sure that you are approaching the matter most effectively.

TRUE STORY

A couple I knew were in a hurry to build. They submitted a permit application and against their designers' advice, regularly contacted the local offices pushing them to issue their decision notice. The local staff became irritated with the level of pressure they applied. The decision was issued without the normal courtesy of making the applicant aware of any issues that needed to be addressed or giving them the opportunity to clarify their design. As was within their power, they moved straight to REFUSAL, thus achieving the double whammy of improving the departments statistical response times and removing an irritating application from their world. The couple could not complain as their wish for a speedy decision had been met (although not how they expected) and they became embroiled in the lengthy and expensive appeals process.

You've got to know when to hold 'em, know when to fold 'em!'

Permit Refusal.

If at all possible, refusal of a build permit is something you should not allow to occur. It is one big headache. Generally, a refusal can only be countered through an appeal process. On the other hand, a withdrawn application provides a chance to amend your application and resubmit it to align with what will be accepted and approved. Simply put, an application that is under consideration has a chance of approval, whereas a refusal can only be overturned by a successful appeal. This is by no means assured and will cause delay while the process is undertaken.

Because of this, it is important to listen carefully to what the planners tell you and judge what the implications are. If there is a reasonable risk you will be refused permission, strongly consider re-drafting your proposals or withdrawing your application until you feel confident that you can progress the application with approval as the likely outcome.

If your application is refused, get specialist advice from a town planner before you respond or appeal. You will need to review the grounds of the refusal with your consultants and carefully consider seeking advice from experts new to the situation.

You have two options: appealing the decision to an independent expert, or submitting an entirely new application that addresses the points given as the reasons for your lack of success.

A withdrawn permit application is a much better position to be in than a refused permit application.

Chapter 7 – Action

- Complete the program
- Work through early stage designs
- Meet the Structural Engineer
- Work through the 'what does it do/what else does it do' list
- Undertake Value Engineering
- Decide on a planning strategy
- Order planning reports
- Submit your permit application
- Avoid a permit refusal

MONEY
Budget & Cash Flow
Finance timings

PLANNING
Up-date status
Planning permit or withdrawl

TEAM
Who can help-what roles?

TIME
Update work schedule

DESIGN
Decide on construction method & look VE
Lifetime homes
Freeze design

GENERAL
What works will you carry out?

CHAPTER 8
SUMMARY

With the Building Permit granted, the game is on. Everything becomes real and commitments are made.

Highlights covered in this chapter include:

- What are the planning conditions?
- Discharging planning conditions
- Consultants appointed to further stages
- Consider a CE

CHAPTER 8

PERMIT GRANTED

'It takes real planning to organize this kind of chaos'.
— Mel Odom

There is a feeling that you have reached a milestone when the approved building permit is issued for your new home. Finally, the official document enabling you to proceed with building your proposed vision. This is the point where obligations are undertaken and orders placed. Your team of consultants, suppliers, contractors and everyone else will want firm commitments from you before they act.

Take a little time to review what your building permit actually says and any clauses included in the small print. As with every other legal document, the devil is in the detail. Most municipalities issue permits with conditions, such as time limits on the validity of the building permit. Review all the conditions and understand how they affect you. For example, work must commence within 180 days of issuance in Plano Texas, otherwise the permit automatically becomes invalid. If the work is incomplete due to suspension or abandoned 180 days after commencement, the permit also becomes invalid.

Next, consider carefully if the permit granted for the new home is within your budget constraints. Read over your proposals in detail to ensure that you feel comfortable proceeding . Are there any nagging doubts that stop you going ahead, or are you uneasy? Compromises can creep in during the permit application process, particularly if you felt you just had to get on with whatever was required for an approved permit, so these steps below will help assure yourself all is in order.

You can reach out to your consultants to clarify details of your plan or whatever it is you are asking them to do in order to move matters to the next stage.

Building Permit Conditions

Building permit approvals may be granted with conditions that will require you to provide further information. Until any such requirements are met, you do not have full approval for your scheme, and the planning department will not be able to issue a building permit. Review any stipulations with your designers, and discuss how to deal with them.

Other conditions will often be included that relate to specific behavior and procedures during the construction process. They may regulate the hours and days you can work so as not to inconvenience neighbors or delivery restrictions and suchlike.

Some local areas require a contribution or raise a levy towards 'green' issues. Or they may issue local infrastructure tax as part of the conditions of planning approval. It is usually a requirement for these charges to be paid before you meet your planning obligations and can commence on to the construction phase.

Owner-builders sometimes have certain exemptions from some of these taxes or levies, but only if the paperwork is meticulously completed and 'approved' before commencement. Ensure all forms are complete, triple checked, and submitted on time. Municipalities do not 'like' giving owner-builders (or any other builders) exemptions from making financial contributions, so there are rules you must follow to the letter to avail yourself of any associated saving. If you are not on top of your paperwork, you may lose the saving and be forced to pay up. Remember, without a building permit, your house becomes unbuildable and, of course, unsaleable.

In the normal course of events, after the permit is granted, the designer, in conjunction with the structural engineer prepare working drawings to seek *building control approval*. This is a good time to meet with key contractors, visit suppliers and consider options. Now is the time to start sequencing and scheduling the construction process, as this will highlight which items are on the critical path and must be treated as priorities.

An initial building inspector's approval is usually part of the building permit application process. You must schedule regular on-site inspections (usually at key stages such as completion of foundations, framing, electrical, etc.) and get various approvals before construction can continue and ultimately have a Certificate of Occupancy issued.

Discharging Conditions.

When all the information has been brought together, you may need to return to the municipal planners or officials and seek a discharge of conditions so that you can commence construction. Often, some conditions can only be met as part of the normal sequence and process of construction at various stages, so these will need to be addressed at the appropriate time.

Dates.

An important condition to note is the dates during which the building permit is valid. During this period, the work must be substantially completed. How you verify that you have completed and what 'substantial completion' means must be clear in your mind, but also meet code definitions, since these matters are locally judged and do vary.

If you realize that construction will likely extend beyond the valid period, generally you will be allowed to apply for an extension. Extensions cannot usually be sought after expiry, as technically it is difficult to extend a non-valid permission. Applications are best submitted before the expiration date has passed. Some states only issue planning permits of a 12-month duration, so local knowledge is all.

> **TIP BOX**
>
> In some states you need to seek permission or exemption from carrying out works unless you are registered with the state contractor's board. For example, in Nevada you must complete an 'Owner Builder Affidavit of Exemption' and undertake to comply with a set of rules around periods you can sell the property and using only licensed contractors. Check your state or province and comply with local requirements.

Planning Compliance.

It is important that you engage with your consultants and discuss the structural design, because different ways of achieving a sturdy structure may change the appearance of the building. If changes are such that they vary the layout or external elevations check with your consultants if you need to have proposed amendments approved by the planners.

Other changes may be non-structural but visually significant (say, changing tile roofing to steel roofing or a large window at the rear changed to two smaller windows). It is important for you to understand whether or not documented amendments are required to maintain your planning permit. A small investment of time and a little research can help you assess which way you wish to proceed.

Chapter 5 'The Players' references lender compliance procedures and how increasing levels of risk aversion are taking hold. Lenders do not take responsibility wherever possible for anything, and actively pass on risk to the borrower. This is not something they hide. They will explain that corporate responsibility goes two ways and they will protect themselves and also in effect protect you from yourself.

This is all well and good and you will provide them with a copy of your planning permit before you are funded to commence. On completion of the home, you will receive a certificate of occupancy and you will probably seek to change your owner-build loan to a cheaper traditional home mortgage.

To access the new loan your lender will send out a surveyor to value the property and if you have not constructed the home in accordance with the original permit this will be flagged as a risk issue. In all likelihood they will not approve your mortgage application until you have regularized your building permit. You are then reliant on the planners retrospectively agreeing to your change(s) and all that will incur. The nightmare that they will not agree is of course always a possibility and this can lead to appeals and extra costs. As suggested in Chapter 2 'Assessing your Plot', for dealing with easements and covenants, if this does become a problem it's possible to deal with the issue of risk of non-compliance by the way of insurance. You may be able to take out an insurance mitigating potential future cost. But this is a messy way of sorting out something that can be managed as part of the process. There is no guarantee that your lender would agree to this insurance, and prefer the matter dealt with by the planners.

As on-site construction progresses, your engineer will visit and inspect. It is important to have the future potential benefit of a satisfied engineer and a satisfied insurance company. Obviously, if he is not satisfied, the installation must be altered until he is. Keep a record and photographs of the work as inspected.

The engineer will produce a design that must be compared against the designer's layouts. This is so any inconsistencies can be recognised at an early stage and the appropriate designs varied. Thus, conflicts in design are eliminated.

Drawings.

Depending on your confidence and previous experience, discuss with your designers the level of detail and information you want documented on the construction drawings. Designers often like to provide full working drawings, which are detailed drawings of how the structure and finishes will fit together and illustrate the finishes; however, it is up to you. More detailed designs may require more detailed drawings, which in turn require more work, and this comes at a higher fee. Bear in mind, more detailed drawings may save time and effort later when decisions about details that have not been documented will need to be made throughout the construction process. In short, this depends on the level of detail that is important to you.

Party Wall Award.

Your designer will be able to advise if your scheme needs *a Party Wall Award* agreed with your neighbours over a party wall (a wall shared directly with a connected neighbor) or party boundary. It is commonly believed that formal written awards are always necessary. This is not the case. If you and your neighbor both agree, you do not need to enter into a formal award. Sometimes both parties informally agree to be reasonable in their dealings with each other. This has to be agreed voluntarily by both parties or else an award may be required.

You, as the person who is working close to your neighbors' property, are responsible for the associated costs to both parties. You meet the full costs and fees associated with their engagement of any independent surveyor. You also must engage your own surveyor to agree an award with their surveyor. This is seen as a way of safeguarding both parties and reducing opportunities for dispute. Both surveyors will confirm the condition of your neighbor's property before you commence works and agree on how the relevant works are to be carried out.

Chapter 8 – Action

- Seek building inspector approval
- Seek Owner-Builder Permit or Exemption
- Deal with building permit conditions
- Ensure the building permit remains compliant
- Agree level of design needed to build works
- Agree methodology of works to comply with Party Wall Award Agreement

CHAPTER 9
SUMMARY

Cost control is crucial in order for any semblance of organization to be created on site. This chapter guides you in the creation of key documents.

Highlights covered in this chapter include:

- List all cost points
- Seek budget costs
- Elemental cost control
- Three types of budget figures

CHAPTER 9

COST CONTROL

'Events, dear boy, events'.
— British Prime Minister Harold McMillan's response to a journalist when asked what is most likely to blow governments off course.

What Will the Cost Be?

Accurate cost projections are needed throughout the process and are a crucial tool for you to deliver the project on time and budget. In this chapter, we will look at common points of failure on building projects.

In the media, large government and commercial projects are often reported as going over budget; costs as 'out of control' when compared to the original predicted completion dates and cost projections. Surely, you think, large projects can afford consultants designing and cost engineering away to ensure financial disaster does not occur. Yes, they can build to time and budget and some of the time this is exactly what they do.

Why then, does this failure occur?

The reasons commonly given as the culprits are:

- Unexpected and unforeseen conditions, particularly under the ground
- Design changes
- Incorporation of high-tech specifications and software
- Availability of skilled labour
- Contractual disputes

- Contractor and delivery issues
- Complexity of design and delivery

Reasons not commonly given, but sometimes found to be responsible, are:

- Lack of leadership
- No collective team-vision
- The project or task is too much for the team undertaking it
- Not sufficient pre-planning
- The project is in itself not viable
- It's a vanity project
- Willful ignorance

There are lots of parallels to be drawn from large projects and a single owner-build home. The process and type of resources needed are the same. The difference is of scale. The smaller scale and smaller resources can work in your favor and allow you to be more successful than the large scale 'professional' project. The larger public contract will have more masters to appease, but in the end, the similarities are overwhelming.

All the pressures we spoke of before will affect the budgets and the eventual costs of the project. By recognizing them before you prepare budgets and apply costs to the build process, you will be more likely to avoid the mistakes so often reported in the media. Take the opportunity to move away from actions that make your design unclear or cause your management of the project to lose focus. You can positively review what you are planning and strategize delivery. You will then be confident you are acting with knowledge, and with this, be confident over your cost allowances.

Unexpected and Unforeseen Occurrences, Particularly Under the Ground.

Unexpected conditions can occur underground, which by their very name are difficult to avoid. They can include soil contamination or remnants of a previous and unrecorded structure. From a cost perspective, the number of surprises can be reduced by ground investigations and research of previous site use. It is always worth asking a seller if they have any soil investigation reports for the site and if they will send you a copy. This information will be useful to your engineer and he will be able to indicate any design issues from the information. Even with this information, a contingency sum should be allowed over-and-above the *ground work cost allowances*.

The good thing about this separate contingency is, its need will be determined at the early part of the project. Once excavations are complete, you will know if it was necessary to draw down on the sum.

Your ground investigations will likely spell out the soil and strata conditions. The fear is, something from a previous era exists, perhaps an old foundation or agricultural structure, like a forgotten well or dump. A hazardous materials audit will identify lead paint, asbestos, etc in existing structures.

A Cultural Heritage Management Plan will identify actions required if you discover relics or remains of previous cultures and historical artefacts.

TRUE STORY

We were building a school and everything was designed for a lightweight single storey structure. It was specified as a strip foundation of 39" (1m) deep by 18" (500mm) wide. All went well until we found very poor soil conditions at one corner of the building. This had not shown up on the geotechnical surveys. We kept digging and found load-bearing strata at 13' (4.0m) deep. We had discovered an old refuse dump! The building inspector and the client's architect both agreed we had to *solid fill* the foundations in this area with concrete. We ended up with a solid foundation deeper into the ground than the building it was supporting went into the air.

This was not efficient; in fact, it proved very expensive, so if the unexpected happens to you, ensure you have a sufficient contingency fund.

Design Changes.

Design changes are choices, and at times expensive ones. After the project design is frozen, design changes by type can be cost-neutral, cost-saving or cost-increasing. The third type are the ones to watch for as they can severely compromise your budget. As long as you balance your budget increase by omitting an item of a similar value, no problem. If not, you'll need to increase your budget to meet the extra cost or amend the change to make it cost-neutral. At least you will have recognized the issue and dealt with it, as opposed to reacting to it later in the project.

Incorporation of High-Tech Specifications and Software.

Be careful of getting sucked in by the glamour of mod-cons or gadgets considered to improve the bragging rights of the home to others. Consider if these features improve the experience of living in your new home… or are they unnecessary glitz? Carefully review the cost of each and every electronic gizmo and prioritise what is necessary and what would be nice. Create a list of these items and keep the costs under close observation. If you can afford them, no problem. If their inclusion makes other necessary items unaffordable, then at least there is a clear choice.

Availability of Skilled Labor.

As the owner-builder, you should draw up a schedule of work. It is a good discipline to allocate each trade or item of work to a known person or company.

It is never too early in the process to talk to contractors and tradesmen about your works and keep them informed of on-site progress as far as it is relevant to them. Always get quotations and budget in as many known prices as you can. Working on an actual quotation is always better than any other figure.

Review your *critical path schedule* to ensure you are ready for contractors. By providing them with regular updates, sufficient notice and a ready-to-go work area, you will greatly reduce possible labour no-shows or delays.

Contractual Disputes.

Keep contracts as simple as you reasonably can. The more complex the contract agreement, the larger the sum the contractor will price into his quotation. He will be concerned of falling foul of the contract and suffering a penalty. The contract, however, has to work. There is no point in an agreement which does not work for both parties, as this is the essence of all agreements. By all parties understanding the agreement and their obligations, the risk of dispute is reduced. Reducing risk will allow the contractor to offer a more competitive price.

Contractor and Delivery Issues.

Pay careful attention to the design elements of all specialist contractor design. Be clear on what they are offering and the options are. Anything 'special' can often mean more expensive, and only through discussion can you fully understand any cost-reducing options available.

Lead-in times from the point of order and sign off to delivery is often extended if the order is categorised as having 'special' features or, as can be the case, just different to their stock standard product. What you are ordering may not even be that special. If you understand their product and the offer, you can sometimes negotiate cost and delivery times without a discernible reduction to the overall quality by accepting their 'standard' finish.

Always confirm any change implications at the end of the design phase and sign off. Design changes may increase the price or extend delivery dates.

On this subject, try to get a fixed date for delivery as opposed to a less explicit number of weeks for manufacture and delivery. Confirmed delivery dates must be fed into the schedule of works to avoid delay.

Complexity of Design and Delivery.

Where more than one designer is involved, there will always be crossover points and compromise. This is initially only with professional consultants, such as principal designer and structural engineers, and is straightforwardly dealt with before the design is frozen at the point of the planning application. After commencement, other suppliers/contractors may have specialist design elements that impact on the approved design or perhaps will conflict with other specialist contractor's designs. It is crucial you stay on top of this because interfaces between the designs can make the build complex.

Complex is never a term mentioned in the same sentence as *economy*, so keep things simple and buildable and you will stop price increases. Be aware of design changes that may compromise permitted work under your planning approval. Discuss the changes with your principal designer if you are in any doubt as to which changes are minor and will not require further approval and which changes will require re-submission to the planners. Moving away from the agreed design can lead to increased costs through delays to the build period or changes to other contractors' works.

Lack of Leadership.

When operations proceed to a plan, they are always smoother than a haphazard approach. Economy is achieved through efficiency and leadership aids efficiency. As project champion, you can help the project to move forward methodically and to a good standard. If you are unable to supervise the works, you must name within your costings who will take supervisory responsibility and how this role will be undertaken. Supervision costs should be allowed within the preliminary section, and this will be spread over the whole project rather than specific trade items.

No Collective Team-Vision.

Everyone needs support, either general or practical. Practical is always better and it is even more valuable if it is targeted. The targeted approach is to empower someone for a specific role you may not excel at. If you need help with accounts, or with site cleaning, or with driving to pick things up, then get help. If you involve team members who can help, then this will make a huge difference; practical support can boost morale and keep you on top of your game.

The vision part comes in with all members of your team knowing what their jobs are and what key objectives you expect from them. Once they understand their role, they can contribute to the team and make a real difference. They can picture their role as a vital part of the whole project. This can be a learning opportunity, which if grasped can benefit all. The team effect can keep the budget on course and make savings across the board.

The Project or Task is too Much for the Team Undertaking It.

This rarely occurs. By taking care over the preceding points, you'll hire a robust team and prevent this problem. Partly constructed properties are occasionally marketed for sale and although an issue in a separate part of the builder's life is usually cited, the real reason can be the build process. The owner-builder was simply overwhelmed and not supported. In my experience, the financial values achieved from a fire sale are a low percentage of the land's value and of the work completed. Under stress, the seller has to take what he's offered and departs the scene well out of pocket.

Be assured that preparation and planning can make all the difference, not trade skill levels. All parts of the project are important and must all be given their fair due. Poor preparation can have a devastating effect on the budgets and lead to disastrous financial consequences.

Insufficient Pre-Planning.

You not only have to budget for the period on-site but for the whole period of the project. This includes the pre-planning stage, which can easily be as long (or longer) than the on-site phases. As soon as you purchase the lot, costs start mounting. These costs include you and your consultants' time on design and selection, as well as the lender's interest charges on borrowed funds.

The other side of the equation is the cost of not sufficiently pre-planning. If you do not plan and scheme, you will not get best value. You must be single-minded and take the planning stage seriously. Poor preparation with the permit application may lead to an inferior permission. Inferior projects, are harder to build, and costlier to maintain.

The Project is in Itself Not Viable.

Project non-viability comes in two main guises. The first arises if you are not sufficiently prepared and so have not realised your design will just not work financially. Your engineer will ensure that all is structurally sound; it is often the cost of the structure and finishes that are the problem. By not going through the project costs in detail, you will simply run out of money. You may put sums to all the items but your budgets do not reflect the costs you are incurring. Your lender will quickly refuse to extend funding, because it seems the golden rule of lending is: never lend money to someone who needs it! They want cast iron guarantees that you can afford to repay them.

The second issue is over-capitalising. This is where the property is too highly specified or over-sized for the plot. This is OK when you are going to stay in the completed home for the rest of your life, with no issues over re-financing or selling. Simply put, you are over-invested in the property; you will not in the short/reasonable term, get the value back in line with what you've expended. It would have been cheaper and easier for you to purchase a completed house in line with local values. The project was simply not viable.

It's a Vanity Project.

Be honest with yourself and determine the reasons you want to build a new home. It is often because you either feel you deserve better, as a reward for your many achievements in other fields, or because you want your family to have the best. This may be admirable, but financially dangerous. Here, you are not making rational decisions based on family needs or increasing your wealth… but on a perceived quality of outcome. This means decisions are made which will invariably increase the costs more than they should.

If you are wealthy and can afford it, so well and good. If it is tough going yet you know what you want, rather than completely compromise, you can budget in phases. This way, you don't have to give up on the dream but rather build the dream in affordable chunks.

Do you want the house to follow the design trend of the 'if you have got it, flaunt it' school of architecture, to make a statement to the world? If so, be careful not to follow the politicians who aim to make an empowering statement to their constituents by building a wonderful bridge from 'nowhere to nowhere'. Make sure your 'bridge' goes from somewhere to somewhere more important. If you cannot rationalise the cost benefit, all will be OK as long as you can afford it. If not, do not do it!

Willful Ignorance.

This is rare but not unheard of. The owner-builder is reckless and wants this house, regardless of who picks up the tab. Often it will not be themselves but rather a patron who will indulge them (perhaps Mum and Dad). They don't know they will run out of funds as they never investigate sufficiently, in case they find out! It was always known that it would exceed budget, but if this was acknowledged early on, it would never have been approved to commence. The person undertaking this act will be unlikely to read this or any other building book. If you are the patron of this behaviour, then act quickly to ensure all costs are diligently provided, before you suffer the consequences of others' actions.

Costs matter if you do not have infinite money.

Costs start accumulating from the bid for a piece of land through to detailed design decisions made during the construction process. If you are committed to meet ongoing payments to a lender, this fact can be crucial. So, accurate actual costs are important.

Cost control is also important, as it not only signals when you are over-spending but also where you can enhance a finish. Often a higher quality and higher cost item can be considered within budget.

What would be ideal is a catch-all method that accurately calculates the cost of the building works. A simple method to guarantee success. No such system exists, as all cost projections are mere predictions of what may occur.

What *is* available are recognized methods of assessing projected costs. Unfortunately, these are all subject to degrees of inaccuracy because what is sought is an expectation of what will happen. And as with any prediction, events occur that will vary the sum allowed for in the prediction. Only by having fixed costs and known conditions could a truly accurate figure be given. Building sites are not close to this! Unexpected events occur with regularity, even becoming the normal condition. This does not mean you do not try to predict costs and create a budget but rather it means *you must try harder.*

You must recognize the inherent issues and try to allow for these inaccuracies within your cost projections. The intention is to control costs so they do not spiral out of control. To do this, we must first create a cost schedule so that budgeted targets can be set.

Basically, the more detailed and researched the projection, the more chance the sum predicted will be within an acceptable percentage tolerance of the final account. Similarly, the more research undertaken into materials, prices and actual quotations from contractors, the better.

The First Problem

The projected build cost information will be based on an assumed house size and approximate average costs. At the time of your offer to purchase the lot, you will not yet have a house design or be anywhere near freezing the scheme in order to submit a building permit application. Although you need to feel confident that you can build to meet the proposed cost constraints.

Your designer will be able to assist on proposed reasonable floor areas.

The Second Problem

Many lenders will not lend anything at all towards the purchase of the lot unless the site is zoned residential and possibly also a building permit is in place. Perhaps some lenders will be moved on this but you must be sure you can secure the purchase funds at closing.

A common response is that you purchase the lot without a lender, using your own funds, and a mortgage is provided for the full amount (or high percentage) of the build cost after issue of the appropriate permits.

The three costing methods that are most suitable for the owner-builder:

- Unit Method
- Superficial Method
- Element Breakdown

Unit Method (Ball Park).

The most basic method of deciding a construction budget is the unit method. You need to have a few basic items of information:

- Purchase cost of lot, including all fees and taxes
- Cost to construct
- Gross Development Value (what is the value of the completed home on this lot)
- How much money can you put into the deal?

At this stage, all figures will be best guesses as many of the allowances will be approximate.

Assumed values.

Purchase of lot	$200K
GDV	$600K

The answer to be determined is: What saving is there in building your own home over buying a similar finished home?

This example leaves $400K before you have spent more on construction than the house is worth on completion. $600K *minus* $200K *equals $400K left over* if you are not seeking a mortgage.

Mortgage.

If a lender is providing finance towards the purchase/build cost, the following is the case if the lender values the (to be completed) house at $600K.

Lenders typically offer mortgages at an amount of between 65% and 90% of the GDV.

This is known as the Loan to Value Ratio (LTV).

Lenders typically offer lower interest rates to lower risk customers.

If you are paying a larger deposit, you reduce the lender's risk.

Low Risk = Lower Interest Charge.

In this case, the lender's offer of borrowing is between $390K and $540K.

$600K x 65% = $390K or $600K x 90% = $540K.

Meaning, you need to find an amount between $60K and $210K as your deposit contribution.

$600K - $390K = $210K or $600K - $540K = $60K.

You must state how much you will put into the deal and how much you propose to borrow.

Basically, you must assess, in the overall scheme of things, what sum you shall allow for construction and added on costs. This, the most basic method of costing, is often the first one an owner-builder will rely upon to give them a guide. Have a conversation with someone you trust about *very* outline costs. You may find this assists to get you to the second stage… although this will only ever be a 'ball park' figure. All the above is only looking at the eventual mortgage position once the house is signed off as complete.

Backtracking a bit, you may need to arrange finance to initially purchase the land, probably without the benefit of your preferred design and building permit. You will need to transfer a deposit on agreement to purchase and be able to access funds at closing. Further funds to carry out the building work will also be needed.

There are lenders who specialize in the owner-build market and fund lot purchase and build costs. Often these are a subsidiary of a larger lender who will transfer your debt to a 'normal' and cheaper mortgage on completion of the project.

There are also higher cost lenders who make funds available on a shorter term basis. They provide bridging finance as a stop gap while you get your other funding in place. These companies charge a premium and are ruthless in chasing down outstanding debt. They will act completely within the law but they will not offer you any comfort if you cannot meet your repayment schedule.

Superficial Method.

The superficial method is a basic calculation of overall costs and is only of assistance at the early stages of a project. It is useful, though, as superficial single rates figures are discussed within the construction industry and appropriate rates are given in owner-build and trade magazines and on the internet. The information must match your actual circumstances and location.

The calculation is worked through by multiplying the floor area ft^2 (m^2) by a sum of money (unit rate). This will tell you how much money the whole build will cost. You will get figures by this method, but the accuracy of these figures is dependent on the quality of information.

The sum given to per square foot (meter) of floor area assumes all floor areas are the same cost to construct. On a 'six of one, half a dozen of the other' basis, an average figure can be taken.

Floor area is taken as the area inside the external walls. No allowance is made for internal walls, staircases, corridors, etc. All the areas are combined into a single sum and multiplied by a monetary figure.

The accepted home build cost ratio figure is multiplied by the floor area and a basic budget figure is given. This figure can be compared to the cost of equivalent completed homes in the area currently on the sales market.

Numbers Don't (Usually) Lie.

According to national census information, the average new build Canadian house is 1948 sq ft (181m^2) and the average new build US house is 2,164 ft^2. (201m^2). I have assumed a house of 2000 ft^2 (186m^2)

The sum of $155 ft^2 ($1668m^2) was given by National Association of Home Builders as an average build cost in the Northeast region, US. Their cost ranged between $100/155 ft^2 ($1076./1668m^2) dependent on region.

Say, 2000 ft^2 (186m^2) completed homes sell for $500K – thus each ft^2 of internal floor has a value of $250 (2,690m^2) including land and build costs. Values across the US and Canada vary greatly and a quick look at Schenctady NY shows complete houses on largish lots for sale for under $100 (1,076 m^2) and over $300 per square foot (3,229m^2). This shows that even in a single community, house prices can have significant variations.

If you add your land purchase cost and your build cost together:
Land Purchase $150K…(This figure is an average assessment)
Land Purchase $150K plus average house size of 2000 sq ft. (2000 x $155) = 150K + 310K = $460K.
This sum needs to be increased to include professionals, OH&S, lenders interest, fees for construction costs, your loss of income etc.

Owner Builder – Total $460K.
Buy Completed Home GDV = $500K.

This assumes that the lenders appraiser indicates a value matching locally available similar homes for sale. A premium for a new home is sometimes applied.

If a tax is payable for the purchase of vacant land or completed houses, then the appropriate figure in your area, state or province needs to be added. This will vary both figures considerably.

Reality Check.

Our example outcome is unclear and unacceptable but is a reflection of the calculated costs and average figures taken from official sources. I have taken the nominal lot purchase figure of $150K. Perhaps this is an incorrect assessment of the market in your area. You need to do your own research in your area and prove to your own satisfaction that you can responsibly afford to enter the owner-build market. Certainly, I could have fudged the figures and provided a more comforting prospect but this section may save you from an unreasonable land purchase and development.

> **TIP BOX**
>
> Custom Builders often do not include everything in their headline sales price. It pays to scrutinize the paperwork and see what is included and what you 'must' pay extra for. You may wish to 'upgrade' because included items may be insufficient for you to enjoy your new home. These extras range from additional power points in each room, carpets, brick paving, letter boxes, full bathroom tiling, fencing etc. This can conceivably add around 10-20% to the initial figure. Be cautious and do not take anything for granted.

In reality, not every square foot (meter) is as expensive to build as every other one. Bathrooms are more expensive to construct per ft^2 (m^2) than bedrooms, and kitchens are more expensive than garages. Basements are more expensive than any other floor level. So, it quickly becomes apparent this method is both open to interpretation and is innately inaccurate.

That said, you need a target figure in order to know if your proposed build ambitions are at all viable, and the basic superficial measurement gives you some clarity over cost projections.

This superficial method can be made more accurate by dividing the areas into room functions and allowing an increased cost for generally higher-cost areas. Non-standard items, such as piled foundations, sedum roofs or air conditioning, or even a high specification 'branded' kitchen can be added separately in order to tweak cost predictions.

The USA regions are different from each other as well as from the Canadian market but the principles remain constant. Local information will provide a local solution.

Elemental Cost Control (Simplified Version).

Creating accurate and detailed elemental breakdowns is very worthwhile and the higher degree of accuracy the better! A CE will have experience and skill honed over many years on many projects producing cost information and the owner-builder undertaking their first project does not have opportunity to fully develop these skills in time for this project. However, for those who wish to take on this challenge, I suggest the following is a responsible approach.

This breakdown can help the other professionals on the team to see how much has been allowed for in the different sections, although you may wish to keep your own counsel over a few cost points, dependent on your relationship with all members of your team.

This is a more accurate method of predicting costs, with more details included over and above the simpler *unit method* and *superficial method*. Its purpose is to produce budget figures, which can then be worked with, monitored and updated.

To create your build cost projection, you'll need to break down items of cost (work) as listed and put target prices against each point. These costs will be a combination of particular items and whole trades or a group of items.

The items are best listed logically, in the order in which they occur. These will be close to the list you created as part of the schedule of works, and it must include all costs. This includes the original purchase cost of the lot and all associated fees and taxes. These amounts can be picked up from the conveyancer's statement.

There are also other set-up costs, which include professional consultants' costs and lender costs, such as valuations and lending fees.

What to Do?

List the building trades sections or items in a point-by-point manner. It's advisable you first create the whole list before filling in sums. If you stop to calculate each item before moving on, you'll likely get bogged down in detail. The list will also provide a good guide to where you are going.

The initial items, such as excavation and soil removal, are difficult to assess. Working out soil bulking is notoriously difficult and so a general sum should be allowed. This will be based on the quantity of the cubic yards (meters) to be excavated.

If you can, seek out a contractor to provide a fixed lump sum for excavations and earth removal and include this amount in your cost schedule. It may be that the groundworks contractor will provide a fixed sum for the machine and driver but the trucks are charged by the load.

Other items, such as foundations, can be better cost estimated or figures taken from quotes. This method continues; count all purchase items, such as windows and doors, and allow a figure for each. With basic drawings, you can get budget costings from specialist contractors, such as plumbers, electricians, etc. and their itemised figures are built in.

Groundworks contractors will often provide a quotation for all works up to and including excavation, drainage and concreting. By grouping these items together, the work may easily be carried out by a single crew and you'd get the continuity of site labor up to DPC level. Everything below this level can be considered as substructure and everything above can be considered as superstructure. The DPC marks a natural dividing point. They may add the carting away of material spoil and charge as per their supplier's invoice, or any combination as agreed. Drainage is carried out by the plumbing contractor, or a specialist drainage contractor. They will be well versed in working alongside groundwork contractors.

Other cost points will be for services supply, say water or electricity. You will probably rely on quotations from a single utility supplier for each supply as they often operate as a monopoly. This eliminates the opportunity to seek competitive prices from different contractors. These costs can also be applied to your spreadsheet.

General costs must also be allowed, including waste and rubbish removal. During the work, a refuse dumpster will likely be needed on site, collecting various types of waste. For this, you must have an allowance that is based on how many dumpsters you estimate will be required each week of the build period. You could project one or two a week, or more, dependent on the work entailed.

Scaffolding and access to site will be required, so you must discuss with contractors what access you must arrange.

Do the bricklayers want three lifts of scaffolding, each lift erected separately as the work proceeds? Will the roofer need a further lift at roof level?

Scaffolding is expensive and risky. It is expensive because as a temporary structure it must be erected to a very high standard and be robust to meet the challenges of a working site. It is risky because after an initial fixed period, the scaffolder will invoice you a *standing hire charge*. The costs multiply as delays occur; the scaffold may not even be used but is racking up ongoing costs.

As it costs a substantial sum to erect and strike a scaffold, taking it away while not in use is not an option. If the scaffold remains onsite for an extended period, it can be worthwhile trying to renegotiate the weekly hire rate with the scaffolder.

Other trades may also require towers or mechanical lifting equipment and this too must be factored in.

There are some costs that are not unexpected; just unknown. Include a sum for unknown costs that are guaranteed to come up during the construction process. This allowance is known as a *'contingency'*. This sum is often assumed as a percentage of the construction costs – often 10%.

All in all, this will be a detailed document, which, tackled one item at a time, is not as difficult to compile as you may first think. This document allows you to drill down to look at your particular build sequence and allow sufficient money to complete your build. You simply work through all the materials required and add them into the overall calculation, including an amount for labor.

Watch Out for Unit Rates.

You may be offered a 'Unit Rate' by a contractor. This is a monetary rate to carry out specified works. This can be a number-per-unit rate or a square rate or cubic area rate. The amount of work completed will be measured on site to calculate how much he will charge and you shall owe.

This can be good, bad, and indifferent. It is good as the contractor feels confident, he will be paid for all the work he completes. It is bad because you have someone working for you without a fixed sum or total cost figure. It is indifferent *if* you know how many of whatever it is, of the unit rate he can possibly complete, giving you an answer before he commences.

There are, however, issues which could possibly arise.

If you are paying for something you cannot genuinely measure, say bulked earth removal, then it is fair that a careful count is maintained and the number of truck loads removed are paid for. The contractor can give you a fixed price, but they will consider a worst-case scenario and then add a bit more 'to be sure'.

If you are paying for something which you can measure, why not just measure it? This can be right and this can be wrong. An example of 'right' is a carpenter hanging doors, complete with door linings, trim, door stop and complete door furniture. As this is a definite list of points easily checked, then simply calculate the number of doors and charge the unit rate per door.

An example of 'wrong' is a fixed price quoted by a carpet layer. It is true that he can provide an area price but he has to buy carpets in certain manufactured fixed widths and lengths. The shape of your floor areas will dictate the amount of waste, or *offcut,* they will be left with. And so, since only by measuring on site or from a drawing can they offer their best price, the simple unit rate will not offer value for money.

Once the cost points are listed, enter all the known and calculable figures.

Often these figures will be 'guestimates', meaning a reasonable budget for a particular item. An example of this would be major appliances, such as a washing machine or a dishwasher. You can check the typical prices of the individual goods, then add them together and round them up to give you an overall budget for the item *Appliances*.

Some items are easier to guestimate than others. For example, electricians will often provide a budget figure per point (light point and power point) and by counting up the points, you can arrive at a budget figure. (It could be by discussion you ascertain if this includes say the meter box or mains supply from the meter or not). The known sums are entered onto a spreadsheet and updated as regularly as possible. Close cost scrutiny allows you to plan and spend your money effectively.

By keeping a close watch on the budget, you can manage one of the greatest stress questions of the owner-building process 'can we afford what we are instructing?' By keeping the process going, at the end you can show real costs and see how well you have fared.

Build cost projection is an amalgamation of known costs and fees, budgeted costs, guestimates and overall percentage figures. As a science, it is not accurate enough but as a budget, it is all that is available until actual sums can be entered.

In many established residential areas, the only way to get vacant land is to demolish an existing property and create a vacant site. So, the cost of demolition must be factored into the budget, including OH&S procedures and checks such as asbestos surveys, demolition planning permits, etc.

If you are intending to employ a single principal contractor and project manage them, employing a professional cost consultant (CE) is advisable. Keeping the parties honest, they will produce a specification, seek tenders, and advise on the procedures going forward.

Specifications.

This document must be clear with precise descriptions of the work and what standards contractors must achieve. When put like this, it seems reasonable; just these points will avoid confusion and follow-on disputes.

The specification supplements the information detailed on the drawings.

According to the Construction Project Information Committee (CPIC), the purpose of a specification is as follows:

- The designers' detailed requirements must be met
- The work can be priced with accuracy
- Products can be ordered correctly and in good time
- The works can be planned, executed and supervised in a controlled manner.

> **TIP BOX**
>
> *What's in a name?*
>
> When a person gives you an approximate cost, it's a *guestimate*.
>
> When they indicate a provisional cost, it's an *estimate*.
>
> When they say their costs should not exceed a certain level, it's a *budget*.
>
> When they provide you with a fixed sum that they undertake to carry out the work for, it's a *quotation*.
>
> When they provide you with a single cost to carry out a specific task, with no option of remeasurement, extras or savings, it's a *fixed price lump sum*.
>
> When they submit their offer at the same time as others in competition, it's a *bid or tender*.

Costs

What is the base information you need to assess if the project is viable? Let's give you an example. The below list assumes you have a site in mind to which you can attribute projected costs:

An Example of a Build Cost Projection Budget

Item	Budget	Total
Property Cost		
Legal Fees		
Purchasers' Costs		
Purchasers' Taxes		
Sales Cost of Previous Property		
	0.00	0.00
Designer		
Engineer		
Planning Consultant		
Secondary Consultants		
Building Insurance		
Temporary Power		
Services		
Permits		
Home Warranty Insurance		
Building Inspection		
Other local Charges		
Lender's Fee		
Lender's Interest Sum		
Lender's Inspection Fee		
Overheads you must carry		
	0.00	0.00
Demolition		
Enabling Works		
Build (per ft²/m²)		
Garages (per ft²/m²)		
Overheads		
Rubbish/Waste Removal		
	0.00	0.00
• *The list gives an indication of possible items.*	Total	0.00

The schedule is broken down into three sections:

Section 1.

Property acquisition costs. It's best to decide if you will only allocate costs strictly attributable to the purchase or if you'll broaden costs and fees to cover items that you must spend to achieve the eventual purchase. For example, if you incur costs visiting the property prior to purchase – are these costs included? The important point is that you decide what is included and what is not. This gives clarity. You can list a point and decide not to allocate a cost. This shows that the item was considered even if no cost was included.

Section 2.

Consultancy and insurances, etc. It is hard to gauge these costs but you must make an attempt and allocate a financial amount. Perhaps try to allocate a ballpark figure. Where they are still listed as 'known unknowns' discuss with your designer what percentage of the project build sum it would be reasonable to allocate to these points.

Section 3.

Build costs. These are the major figures and the ones with the greatest variance. Decide how you are going to tackle this and give it the best shot that you can. The more you work through this, the higher accuracy you will achieve.

Be prepared. This is the best defence to avoid unexpected and financially painful situations.

You do not want to talk yourself out of building your own home and the more prepared you are the better placed you shall be. Obviously, this schedule just has general points listed and you must include items to match your project.

PHILIP FITZPATRICK

> **TIP BOX**
>
> **The Golden Thread of Information**
>
> A verbal contract is not worth the paper it is not written on.
>
> Keep good records – from the beginning.
>
> Written quotations from providers allow accurate orders to be placed.
>
> Clear orders generate clear delivery notes.
>
> Clear delivery notes make approval of invoices a lot easier.
>
> Complete paperwork gives accurate costs.
>
> Tax is easiest saved if you can prove cost.
>
> Exact costs as you proceed allows for good budgeting.
>
> Good budgeting allows for accurate cost projection.
>
> Accurate cost projection enables cost-based decisions to be made with knowledge.
>
> Cost based decisions allows clear instruction.
>
> Clear instruction avoids the largest reason for disputes.
>
> Avoiding disputes saves money, time and stress.
>
> Avoiding the distractions of dispute improves the quality of the build.
>
> The benefits are negated if you do not keep complete sets of basic information.

Chapter 9 – Action

- List all costs incurred to date
- Determine the relevant charges by levy or tax?
- What consultants fees are still to be incurred?
- Create a list of work
- Provide specific details - attach drawings
- Seek prices from contractors
- Put sums against each item
- Include a contingency sum
- Include for cleaning up and waste removal
- What costs will you incur in carrying out the works?
- Create a working budget and cash flow

MONEY
Budget & Cash Flow
Finance timings

PLANNING
Discharge planning conditions

TEAM
What enabling works need to be done?

TIME
Update work schedule

DESIGN
Specialist advice
Seek quotations
Instruct working drawings
Building control approval

GENERAL
Identify contractors

CHAPTER 10
SUMMARY

Money management skills are not nice to have; they are fundamental

Highlights covered in this chapter include:

- Cost control - if you feel you cannot personally keep an updated schedule, find a volunteer to take on this vital role
- You must be up to date with the paperwork, or suffer the consequences
- Carry out a financial audit *on yourself*
- How to prepare a loan application
- Keep an eye on your own credit rating

CHAPTER 10

MONEY

'The person who doesn't know where his next dollar is coming from usually doesn't know where his last dollar went'.

– Unknown

First, Get Funding

One of the many 'first' things the Owner-Builder needs is sufficient funding to thrive. Without sufficient funding, the project will fail under the weight of its own debt. Without a reliable and predictable flow of money, your project is dead!

There are many options for funding, and they all come with different risk levels and different costs. As an owner-builder, you will need to work with whatever is available.

Obviously, the amount of debt you take on will depend on your circumstances, your attitude to debt and your ability to service debt.

Start Up and Organization.

You need 'start-up' money and this is best funded by yourself and family. You should set yourself up properly in a business-like fashion, with a computer ready to use spreadsheets and e-mail. An office space with a filing system is advisable. In it, you can safely store the information gleaned at building exhibitions and wherever else you have found inspiration for your new home.

When you travel to view lots, take time to investigate them before you start spending at-risk funds with lawyers and consultants. This is akin to setting up a business as far as outgoings are concerned, except with a crucial difference. You will never have profits returning to you. Your home will not be a profit center.

This is the point where you need to be aware of cash out and cash balanced so that bills can be met. There are overheads with any venture and these need to be covered. Keeping with the business analogy, as businesses grow, so does their need for money. Your owner-built home will be the same. Your enlarged commitments will need to be fed by a constant supply of available money.

You will need to be aware of what 'events' could take place and allow a contingency to cover the unexpected, although not the unforeseeable.

Rain may not be expected tomorrow, but it is foreseeable rain will fall at some point.

Insurance covers most catastrophic natural disasters but there are always matters you will need to pay for out of your own pocket. Even ordinary matters need a large financial outlay. This can be, for example, tools and access equipment. These items need replacing through natural wear and tear. After going over the sums, you may decide to buy your own equipment rather than pay an ongoing hire cost.

Lenders.

When applying for loan, you will be in competition for funding, where everything is assessed. Indeed, the visual standards of presentations and your organizational skills have to impress and if possible look sophisticated. You need to look professional in your application, understand what your message is and ensure it's clearly communicated.

This sounds more corporate than owner-builders think they should have to be; but you must be clear on what you are doing and how you will achieve it. If you are not clear, how can your lender be clear? This self-clarity will improve your application and increase its chances of success.

Funding.

Funding is more than budgeting on a larger scale than usual—it is the backbone of the project.

You first need to establish you are solvent and what your assets are. To help with this, all lending institutions provide downloadable forms to try to gauge the state of your finances. From this snapshot, you'll be able to determine where you are financially, as you will list your assets and obligations. Below are some guiding questions.

Q. If you are going to physically construct your own home, will you be able to maintain your current income level or will it be affected?

Q. How do you intend to manage the project… and will management fees need to be included in the costs?

Q. Do you have a property that has a realizable value? As long as you are prepared to raise funding with it, either by selling or mortgaging (via equity), then this value should be included.

To be clear, if you are not prepared to raise funds against an item, then as far as this exercise is concerned, this value cannot be included. Realisable assets are physical and saleable items the lenders can rely upon should the need arise.

The objects that lenders like most are unencumbered property. If this is not possible, then a property with a small mortgage and a reasonable retained value still available, may be acceptable. Lenders will not lend to the full value amount of a pledged property but take a view on the overall Loan to Value Ratio (LVR).

If you can access family or other money, then this too should be included. But there is a caveat; if you are receiving funds from a family source you must make it clear if the borrowed sum has to be repaid before the build is complete. In addition, a new house will need to be complete and signed off as habitable before you will be able to re-mortgage.

All lenders like to position themselves at the front of the repayment queue and will not allow others to go before them as preferential debtors.

If you are not sure about any of this, or even if you are sure, it's good practice to seek advice from a suitably-qualified financial or legal consultant.

What Can I Afford?

Can I afford to carry out the project? is a basic question. Obviously, you need to consider the total cost of the project, and calculate how much money you'll need at each stage, to answer this effectively.

The points to be covered are:

- What do I have available and how much can I borrow?
- Cost of land, plus taxes and other ancillary costs?
- Cost of design and building permit?
- Cost of construction?
- Other known costs
- Contingency

Take the information from the asset sheet you've filled in for your lender to provide an indication of your financial worth. This may well be a negative figure if you have a mortgage on an existing property.

Add to this figure any funds you can raise by sales or from family means. This should give you a new total. If you intend to sell an existing mortgaged property and realize a greater sum, then also include this. This sum should give you a base projected amount of assets.

With this information your proposed can indicate what level of borrowing is reasonable in your circumstance for an owner-build project.

In other words, the lender should be able to pre-qualify your application. This does not guarantee you will get the money, it means you are seen as someone worth talking to about lending the money.

Ratios.

The lender will be interested in the proposed:

- Mortgage repayment-to-income ratio (RTI). What ratio of your gross monthly income will the proposed loan payment be?
- Total debt-to-income ratio (DTI). What ratio of your gross monthly income will all your debts combined be? (Total debt obligations divided by monthly income).

> **TIP BOX**
>
> If you scrutinize your current and foreseeable financial position you should be able to list and identify all your debts. If in debt, can you modify how you live and look to get rid of the most expensive debt first? Lenders are often reluctant to lend to those considered at 'higher risk' in some market cycles this can mean those with a DTI between 36–49% and during most market cycles those over 50%.

Loan to Value ratio (LVR). What ratio will the loan be to the value of the completed home?

Lenders take a view on all the above and break down matters such as your *front end ratio*, which looks at your current housing costs, such as mortgages and insurances, and your *back end ratio*, which includes all your monthly bills, including child support and credit cards.

Check your credit rating before you approach a lender, so you can fix any errors before they become an issue.

If you are in any doubt, seek professional financial advice.

TRUE STORY

We were having a rough time with 'averages'. We had been nominated for two bids but had not made the final cut on either of them. This was annoying, as they were both good clients. One, a large national distribution center where they were concerned with quality more than price and the second, an iconic building. It seems a company with a very similar sounding name to our company (in a different part of the country) had suffered from financial difficulties. Rather than the project leads informing us of the issue, we were not given the opportunity of being involved. We only found out later that our credit rating was coming up with incorrect information. It was not fair, but we had not subscribed to a credit agency up-date service to prevent this.

There is at times wrong information out there and if you do not correct it, no one else will.

Where Can I Get Funding?

Funding is available from lenders who position themselves in the owner-build market. You may well get the best deals from those institutions which recognize the needs of the owner-builder and offer suitable financial products.

You can find out which institutions are interested in offering you finance by attending building exhibitions, checking magazines and online. Financial advisors/brokers can assist with this and usually have contacts to go to on your behalf. If you have a long-term relationship with a lender, it's always worthwhile approaching them to see if they can assist.

After speaking to a few lenders, or a financial advisor who deals with more than one lender, you should have an indication of your maximum budget. In an ideal world you will have approval from a lender to approve an owner-build loan, with the intention it is transferred to a mortgage on completion of the project.

Grants.

One issue to check out is if there are any grants or Feed-in Tariffs available for your proposed property. You may initially think this is something to pursue later, but why wait? This input could effect on your design and budget.

Governments are increasingly focused on eco-friendly measures for certain energy-saving features in homes. Serious financial grants are available in some areas and states. These consist for example of one-off payments towards the purchase of a solar PV system, linked to attractive low-interest loans, often repaid over a 20-year plus period. Other schemes may be available in your area. This support can critically affect your cash flow. Reviewing this information and bringing it all together should provide you with a maximum budget figure.

Cost of Land Plus Taxes and Other Ancillary Costs?

Farmers and the like often already have a lot available and may forget the concern of purchase costs. The principle is: if it incurs no immediate cost, you need not include it. If it has a cost, this should be entered into the equation. If you are purchasing the land, then all costs, such as lawyer's fees, mortgage costs and taxes, should all be listed and included. If you are not sure what the level of costs will be, then ask your lawyer for a fee proposal.

Cost of Consultants and Services.

If the lot requires a change-of-use permit before a dwelling can be constructed, this cost needs to be included. Every local planning office requires a fee before they will consider a building permit application. The local office will publish this fee on its website. A larger sum will also need to be paid to your consultants to collect the information necessary to submit an application.

You should discuss in detail with your lead professional consultant what information will need to be compiled and by whom. The whom could well be a combination of the consultants listed as your team. It is important to get an outline cost from all the consultants so you can determine what the total sum to submit the permit application will be. If you need insurance, or an OB permit/exemption or the like, the costs should be recognised and a sum put forward to be included in the budgets.

How Do I Apply for Funding?

The more professional you appear from your presentation and documentation, the more successful you will be at raising funds. If you are not personally experienced at writing and compiling documents, seek out someone who can help.

As with all aspects of the build process, clarity is also essential in the financial world.

When applying to a lender, you need to make the case for your competence and financial stability. They will want to see if you have considered various aspects of the project and are interested in your ability to communicate what it is you want to achieve, how you will manage it and how the deal stacks up. They will especially want to see your plan to repay your loan on completion of the works and at the appropriate time, move onto a suitable home mortgage. I am suggesting this is information you provide in addition to the lender's application form. This should all be included within your loan application pack. Your financial advisor may be also able to offer guidance in this regard.

How Does Owner-Build Funding Work?

Funders for owner-build projects work in a slightly different way to a normal mortgage scenario. The lender wants confirmation you have a full and complete understanding of the task ahead and they want to see a method of 100%

repayment. What is different is, they want full repayment on completion of the house. The lender may offer 'normal' mortgages as well, which they could transfer their owner-build mortgage to later. Whatever the situation, they will want to see you have sufficient equity and value in the property on completion of the works in order to take out a normal mortgage, thus repaying them. What many owner-builders do not realise is the increased repayment costs charged by lenders for building loans over 'normal' home mortgages. To the lender the risk profile is greater and therefore the rate applied is higher.

The owner-build loan should only be in place during the timeframe of the build project. Plan to transition to a cheaper loan as soon as you can.

Cash Flow.

The lender will also want to pay funds to you in *tranches* as you proceed with the works. They will base payments on your application to the monitoring surveyors, who in turn will produce valuations after an on-site inspection. So, you are paid for progress achieved; they will not fund you in advance. This means planning your payments for materials and labour around their valuations by way of a cash flow schedule.

A cash flow is a schedule of how much funding you predict you will have in place at set points, usually month ends.

This is created in the first instance by listing the items shown on your schedule of work and then producing a cost estimate for each item listed. This estimate predicts how much money is needed to meet your expenses as work and time proceeds. You next produce a schedule of money spent during each month, based on the work you expect to progress during that month. The work items do not have to be completed during each month; a percentage assessment of the amount completed can be acceptable. If you need to pay a deposit, this should be indicated as a cost in line with when the expenditure is scheduled to occur.

This can be a crucial tool in smoothly progressing your build. After all, if you do not have sufficient cash in hand, you cannot meet your payment responsibilities. Also, many specialist manufacturers require deposits at order placement and sometimes full payment before delivery.

Credit.

You will need to balance your budgets and have sufficient funds to meet obligations when they become due, in advance of receiving payment from the lender.

Perhaps you can make the case to the monitoring surveyor to include actual advance-payment-required invoices and so these amounts are allowed in your application. The lender, however, may feel this does not provide the level of comfort needed, since effectively the materials are not on site and therefore not in your control.

A real benefit can be realised by seeking out a good local builder's supplies and lumber yard who can provide a wide range of goods, either in stock or by special order. If you approach them early in the project and indicate you will place orders through them regularly throughout the build, you could be approved for a line of credit. Then you are not due to pay for goods until the end of the following month. This is known as a monthly (30-day) account.

By careful planning, you can achieve good cash flow results. Do this by ordering goods early in the month's cycle and you'll effectively get nearly two months free credit. By the time the invoice is due, the lender will have deposited the funds into your account.

If local merchants will not offer a credit account, you can seek a large overdraft facility with a credit card provider. But you must be tenacious in paying this off before the due date, as the rate of interest charged by credit companies is considerably higher than other usual lending methods. You must be wary of running up high-interest-rate loans; a high level of competence will be required if you are not to pay a very high cost for credit.

To an extent, your contractors also offer you credit. You may not appreciate it as *credit*, but they attend site and provide materials and labour, none of which you have to pay for on a daily basis. In the short term, they fund your build cost. This is a credit line you must not abuse as smaller companies can only go so far before they too need funds to meet bills.

Scheduling.

A good way of dealing with this is to schedule your contractors' payments based on your payment cycle from your lender. As part of your cash flow schedule, you must agree to a payment procedure with your lender. This should stipulate how often the monitoring surveyor will prepare valuations. This payment document provides you with two pieces of crucial information:

The dates you must submit your valuation to the monitoring surveyor.

You should determine from the monitoring surveyor how many days in advance of their visit you need to submit your application. Then, you can tell your contractors the dates they need to submit their payment applications to you, so their invoice amounts are included as part of your application. The monitoring surveyor will not usually want to see the contractor's actual invoices; they will want an indication of percentage of works complete.

The dates you receive draw down payments.

You should determine how long the payment from the lender typically takes after the valuation is submitted for payment. This will allow you to schedule payments to your contractors.

Materials Off-Site.

Sometimes, a contractor will need to order specialist machinery or equipment for your project. The manufacturer will want a deposit and full payment before delivery and the contractor will ask you to fund this to him so he can secure the goods on your behalf. The pitfall with this is, you are funding an intermediary to place an order. If either the intermediary or the manufacturer ceases trading before delivery, you could be out of pocket, not receive the goods and be left with little legal recourse.

A way around this is for you to pay the manufacturer directly on behalf of the contractor, so the contractual relationship is between you and the specialist supplier. You can also request the goods, prior to delivery, are labelled as your property. In the event of any cease of trading issues, the goods are then not caught up in the mix. They remain your property.

What am I Liable to Pay For?

Owner-building is expensive in lots of ways that are often not initially considered. There are the obvious items to be paid for and other costs less obvious that may be required, dependent on your actual circumstances.

You must place a figure on how much you need to borrow, and this can only be arrived at after completing key parts of the information-gathering process. It's a 'chicken and egg' situation, as you cannot allocate costs to a project you have not quantified, and you must value the project prior to quantifying, to confirm if it is viable.

Feasibility.

Evaluating the feasibility of building your own home is a process to indicate if it makes financial sense. In simple terms, you need to produce certain information and assess if it seems reasonable. If so, you can move onto further stages and keep increasing the accuracy of your proposal.

Feasibility analysis is important because the mortgage provider also needs assurances. If you fail to make your re-payments, they can, as a last resort, repossess your property. They are then re-paid the money outstanding on the loan via a forced sale. They need evidence of remaining equity after everything has gone horribly wrong.

Simple Accounts.

It is important for you to record and maintain a simple set of accounts from the outset. A spreadsheet should be sufficient. This will allow you to chart your progress and keep on top of escalating costs. You should regularly review and update the figures.

This record will act as a guide. When considered in the context of overall budget, it will be an invaluable tool in the specification and decision-making process. If you feel this is something you cannot personally keep updated, find a volunteer to take on this vital role.

Every item you are going to spend money on, every amount of money spent because of the project, is to be included. Where you consider an item but do not intend to spend money on it, it should still be noted, and if appropriate, a zero placed against the item. This is to show you have considered this item and not just missed it out.

Recording costs should begin immediately. If you go to view a site, even if you do not purchase, then any costs directly attributable to the trip should be included.

Personal Insurance.

It is worth seriously considering personal insurance. This can be life assurance/income protection or key person insurance. Should an incident occur which results in your injury or death, even away from the site, how would your family cope with the financial turmoil? Lenders do sometimes require this type of insurance as part of their finance offer. Your financial advisor should be able to assist.

Cash is 'King'.

In negotiation, nothing encourages discounts as efficiently as prompt payment. Competent financial management means you can promise speedy payment. Often you will see bargain prices for goods on the Internet or at builders' merchants only available for a limited time. Major savings can be made by having funds available.

Other Known Costs.

Try to include any other known costs. These may include items such as lender's set-up fees or demolition permissions if an existing structure is to be removed prior to construction. Think of things like site entrance costs, say if you require the local authority to remove bushes or construct a vehicle cross-over on the sidewalk from the roadway to the site. There can be a whole range of issues which need a cost allocation.

All these figures should be compiled to give you a budget figure and this will assist you in your review if the owner-build approach is a reasonable way for you to proceed.

It is also a good check to assess the value of your house when works are complete. It is comforting to know it will be worthwhile investing the time and effort to owner-build and discover the tangible value that awaits you on completion.

Compliance.

Many lenders are 'controlled' by compliance officers. Their 'official role' is to ensure the company does not act in any way outside of lending laws, regulations or criteria. The lenders are aware that government bodies and the media have in recent years portrayed them as snaring the unsuspecting public in debts to bolster stakeholders' profits. In reality, the compliance officer's job in life is to follow procedures to ensure lenders' risks are reduced. They are to avoid losing money and to avoid having a borrower to chase for repayment. In the current environment, they seem to raise all sorts of marginally relevant queries. These are all aimed at reducing their company risks to negligible amounts. You have to stick with this process and answer all their points faithfully and honestly no matter how pointless some of the questions seem.

> **TRUE STORY**
>
> I have often in passing discussed with various developer's, different lenders' attitudes to funding projects. It is remarkable how often we have had funding approved from a particular lender when others reported that getting funding there was 'mission impossible'. I believe this is because the others have not listened and focussed on the actual questions asked.
>
> If you provide a comprehensive answer and a logical approach, you are much more likely to succeed. You may think, *fair enough, I bet the others got funding elsewhere so what does it matter?* You would be correct, but it does matter. You want funding from the most competitive lender as it means you pay less back in interest. These sums can be significant.

Loan Applications.

These important documents should be bound or neatly presented in a folder. Take at least two copies to give to the lender and offer to assist after the meeting by forwarding an electronic copy. This gives you an excuse to follow up after the meeting and keep in contact. All the sections below should be on separate pages.

Cover Sheet.

This should give your name and address and the address of the project, the month and year. You can choose, if you wish, to put the lender's name to personalize the cover, and possibly a CAD image of the completed project.

Contents Page.

To be included if the document is over 6/8 pages long. Each topic should be listed with a page number. Appendices should be separately listed at the end.

Introduction.

This is the section where you outline your project and what it is you are trying to achieve. Try to stick to a single page as the lender only wants a flavour. Who are you and what skills do you and your partners bring as champions of the build process? Include any relevant qualifications or background, even if it is not directly in construction. They want to see competence.

You can talk about the location; the benefits of local public transport and the popularity of the residential area. Mention if the site has planning permission for a dwelling, or if not, what your plans to get planning permission are. Confirm the current planning designation for the site. If appropriate, you can mention the average sale prices for properties in the local area (recent ones).

Team Page.

List the names and contact details of your team. It is important the lender appreciates you have professional backup and advice. Provide the practice name, address and full contact details of the named person you are dealing with.

- Architects/Designers
- Engineer
- Building Inspector
- Planning Consultant
- OH&S Consultant
- Accountant
- Lawyer etc.

The Project.

Be factual and produce specifics:

- Lot size
- Floor area
- No. of bedrooms
- Type of construction
- Type of heating
- Appendix of floor plans and elevations

Cost Projections.

- Schedule of values
- Cash Flow schedule
- Financial Plan
- Value of project when complete
- Schedule of works – copy of bar chart
- Risks & Responsibilities – statement showing you have considered what needs to be done

Conclusion.

This is where you sum up the benefits of the project and your delivery of the scheme. It is also where you allude to risks you have assessed that are universal to any project. The lender is well aware of the risks and wants to see how you considered these, along with your position and strategy.

Indicate your intention to reside in the property, but if there was a change of plan, emphasise that you would have achieved sufficient value to repay the lender and make a small profit.

Lenders are impressed if you are on top of your project and can clearly explain your proposals on all fronts. Not many applicants will provide such a comprehensive document.

A well-thought-through scheme will be favored. You should only make verifiable claims, as if you state something challengeable, it makes the whole document suspect. This factual approach will make your application stand out and give confidence to a lender. It will also discipline you to produce a viable proposal with a very good chance of success.

Finally, mention planning again. If the site does not have current planning permit, what is the planning status? Can you show an escape route if approval is not granted? For example, are you buying the site for a value which represents its current value and you could re-sell at this price? Not having a current planning permission is a difficult sell to many lender's and most will not fund a site for a newly built home until a planning permit is issued.

Loan Application.

Complete and include a copy of the lender's loan application form. Complete this in as much detail as you can. As it is 'their' document the lender will obviously be familiar with all the parts and a well answered document will be pleasing to the reviewer.

Construction Phase.

After securing funding from a lender, you have a guarantee you can meet the project's financial commitments. This allows you to commence works. The documents you submitted to the lender as part of your application become 'fixed' as far as your lender is concerned. They represent what you promised to undertake to deliver the completed project.

These documents can be expanded to become very useful as works progress. Updated and expanded, they become aids to the Project Management and financial administration of the project. The schedule of works can be updated to include actual commencement and completion dates. The schedule of values can be expanded to become the written form for the application of payments from the lender's monitoring surveyor. The cash flow schedule can be updated before commencement and revisited for each monthly drawdown payment application and the Financial Plan morphs into an ongoing Cost Report.

All these documents provide you with the information needed to guide the project by giving you accurate, readily updateable forecasts. This allows you to maintain balance in the project and come out knowing where you are financially.

TRUE STORY

Many years ago, I attended a building seminar at which they provided a handout, listing items a lender would like to see included in a loan application. As I was in the midst of my first loan application, I faithfully provided every piece of suggested information.

A year later, I met my 'new' bank contact for a second loan. The loan officer asked me if we had met before, as I seemed familiar, and we both agreed we had never previously met. Then it came to him: my previous application had been used as the bank's national in-house example of a loan application. This, they declared, was what a good loan application looked like!

> So, by simply following advice and delivering on it, I went to the top of the class. It made me wonder why everyone else did not use a checklist. After all, it helped the application to be successful.
>
> Lenders want to lend to competent people, so help them to agree that you are competent!

Chapter 10 – Action

- Make cost control a priority
- Update your cash flow projection
- Keep all orders, delivery notes and invoices safe
- Prepare a comprehensive document for your lender
- Tie in contractors' payment dates to match your cash flow

CONCLUSION

'Talent wins games, but teamwork and intelligence win championships'.
— Michael Jordan

The owner-build world is tough. You have not started building yet, but you feel as if you have been through the wringer just getting a building permit to actually build something. It is important that you're fired up to build this home as it is right for you and your family.

You will, by this time, have professional advisors in place and if you feel they are the right team to deliver this project, then move forward with confidence. If you instinctively feel that all is not quite right, then this is the time to move things around. This is a natural break. If you are not sure, discuss options confidentially with other members of the team or other trusted advisors.

Before you plunge into frenzied activity, take this chance to review and take stock. Confirm the funding is still in place from the lender and think hard about how much the build and its landscaping will really cost. Consider talking to a quantity surveyor/cost consultant to arrive at a realistic sum.

Run through your plans of how you intend to tackle the project and who (by name) will be responsible for what. Look at every line of The 1-Page Owner-Builder Plan and assure yourself you are on the right track.

When the weather and seasons are right and you feel 'this is it', have faith and get on with it. If you take all the precautions advised by your professionals you will soon be in a good position to call yourself an accomplished 'owner-builder'.

GENERAL GLOSSARY

Acrylonitrile-butadiene-styrene (ABS)	Material used to manufacture rigid plastic plumbing pipes.
Air Rights	The ownership of space above a building.
Anthropometrics	Measuring 'typical' humans for design purposes.
Artificial Intelligence (AI)	Artificial Intelligence (AI) is intelligence demonstrated by machines with a level of reasoning or knowledge. This often allows objects to be manipulated or moved.
Augmented Reality (AR)	Augmented Reality (AR) is often confused with VR, although the key difference is that the computer-generated information enhances perception of reality and is not completely based on virtual information.
Austenitic Stainless Steel	Type of Stainless Steel (SS) which is non magnetic and has a high resistance to corrosion.
Back Land	Land that does not have "street frontage" - accessed by a secondary road or lane.
Battleaxe	Back land which opens out in a 'battleaxe' shape.
Bridging Finance	Temporary loan to alleviate a specific financial need.
Brownfield	A site with history of previous construction.
Buildability/ Constructability	Integrate construction techniques to make the build simpler and more efficient.

Building Control Approval	Approval that all is built to national and local codes/standards.
Cesspool	A tank which collects effluent.
Competent person	A person who can identify hazards and has authorization to take action.
Compliant Permission	A planning permission designed around the regulations.
Computer Aided Design (CAD)	A digital technical drawing computer program.
Covenants	A limit or guide to future development.
Critical Path	A sequence of operations to most efficiently guide works.
Cut-in Sites	A site that lends itself to a house being built into an existing hill or slope.
Dead Load/Live Load	Dead Load - Weight of structure. Live Load - Weight of people or stored equipment or furniture.
Defects List	List of defect works aka Punch List or Snag List.
Designed for Manufacture and Assembly (DFMA)	An item designed for both ease of manufacture and assembly.
Discharging Conditions	Compliance with planning conditions.
Dormer Windows	A window that protrudes from a sloping roof.
Drywall	Sheet of gypsum plaster covered with paper, aka plasterboard, sheetrock, wallboard, gypsum (wall) board.
Earth Sheltered	A partially earth covered home.
Easements	A right to crossover or shared access to a piece of land.
Enabling Works	Works carried out to allow other works to occur.
Ergonomics	Efficiency is considered in design.

Firring Piece (Furring US)	A wedge shaped batten fixed to produce a fall to a level surface.
Flood Plain	Land prone to flooding.
Goal Gradients	A perception of advancement that encourages achievement.
Green House/Green Construction	Environmentally responsible construction.
Greenfield	A plot previously undeveloped except for agricultural use.
Hardwall	An undercoat plaster for use on masonry.
Hope Value	A value increased by expectation.
Invert Level	The level of the lowest internal surface of a drain.
Land Reclamation	Creating 'dry' land from raising the height or pumping out water from a marsh or river/sea bed.
Land Rehabilitation	Environmental remediation returning land to previous condition.
Leverage (Lever)	Using borrowed capital for investment purposes.
Lifetime Homes	Design that can be altered to accommodate physical change in occupants.
Method Statement	Written document describing the process of a specific task.
Modern Methods of Construction (MMC)	Homes constructed offsite in 3D modules.
Neutral Air Quality	A level of design and build that does not reduce current air quality.
Option Agreement	A legal document that outlines a possible enforceable option.
Outline Advice	Advice that in principle indicates what should be acceptable and achievable.
Owner - Build	Built by the property owner.

Penetrations	Holes made by services through a finished surface e.g. floor or roof.
Performance Gap	Difference between predicted and actual performance.
Plat Maps	A map showing boundary locations and important local information.
Pods	Modules produced through volumetric construction.
Punch list	Defects list.
R-Value	A measure of how well a material resists heat conduction.
Radon Gas	Radioactive gas that naturally occurs underground.
Reduction Creep	Reduction in scope of a project.
Residual Valuation	Process valuing the a development when complete.
Restricted/Unrestricted planning	Use is either restricted to a specific use or without any pre-determined restriction.
Robotics	Design and operation of robots.
Scope Creep	Incremental increase in scope of a project.
Sedum	A large variety of flowering plants- used as a roof covering.
Self-Build	Building for one's self. See Owner-Build.
Septic System	A septic tank treats the effluent and requires a suitable local outfall.
Slump Test	A measure of the consistency of fresh concrete.
Smart Home Technology (SHT)	Using automation in a residential setting.
Snag Sheet	See Defects List.
Spacers	Plastic or concrete device that sets a distance between rebar sheets or from the external surface.

Structural Members	Primary load bearing components.
Subdivision	A site divided to take more than a single home.
Sump	A low point to collect matter by gravity.
Sustainability	To avoid depletion of a resource.
Three Dimensional (3D)	Made in a solid form (Height x Width x Depth).
Tranches	Divided into parts, especially money.
U-Values	A rate of heat transfer through a material or structure from inside to outside.
Virtual Reality (VR)	A simulated feeling and look of what something would be like.
Volumetric/Modular	Constructing 3D units in factory conditions.
Water Run Off	Water flowing over the ground surface.
Virtual Reality (VR)	A simulated feeling and look of what something would be like
Volumetric/Modular	Constructing 3D units in factory conditions.
Water Run Off	Water flowing over the ground surface.

ABBREVIATIONS

3D	Three dimensional
4IR	4th Industrial Revolution
ABC	A Builders Companion
ABC (2)	Always Be Careful
ABS	Acrylonitrile-butadiene-styrene
ACM	Asbestos Containing Materials
ADA	Americans with Disability Act
ADR	Alternative Dispute Resolution
ADU's	Accessory Dwelling Units
AFSS	Automatic Fire Suppression Systems
AI	Artificial Intelligence
AI (2)	Architects Instruction
AIA	American Institute of Architects
ANSI	American National Standards Institute
APA	American Planning Association
APHA	Australian Passive House Association
AR	Augmented Reality
BAL	Bushfire Attack Level
BCA	Building Code of Australia
BER	Building Energy Rating
BIM	Building Information Modelling
BSI	British Standards Institute
CAD	Computer Aided Design

CAV	Community Asset Value
CBN	Canadian Brownfields Network
CC&Rs	Covenants, Conditions and Restrictions
CIOB	Chartered Institute of Building
CIP	Canadian Institute of Planners
CLT	Cross Laminated Timber
CMHC	Canada Mortgage and Housing Corporation
CPSF	Cost per square foot
CPVC	Chlorinated Polyvinyl Chloride
DC/AC	Direct and Alternating Current
DEAP	Dwelling Energy Assessment Procedure
DER	Dwelling Emission Rate
DFMA	Designed for Manufacture and Assembly
DTIR	Debt to Income Ratio
DWV	Drain Waste Vent
ECI	Early Contractor Involvement aka IPD
EGNH	EnerGuide for New Homes
EMF	Electromotive Force
EOI	Expression of Interest
EPC	Energy Performance Certificate
ESD	Environmentally Sustainable Design
FES	Future Energy Scenarios
FF&E	Furniture, Finishes and Equipment
FFL	Finish Floor Level
FHA	Federal Housing Administration
FRR	Fire Resistance Rating
FSC	Forest Stewardship Council
GDV	Gross Development Value
GIS	Geographic Information Systems
HEMS	Home Energy Management System
HERS	House Energy Rating Scheme

HOA	Homeowners Association
HVAC	Heating, Ventilation and Air Conditioning
IBC	International Building Code
IPD	Integrated Project Delivery aka ECI
IRC	International Residential Code
KoP	Kit of Parts
KYC	Know Your Client
LEED	Leadership on Energy and Environmental Design
LEP	Local Environment Plan
LINZ	Land Information New Zealand
Low E	Low Emissivity Glass
LVR	Loan to Value Ratio
MBIE	The Ministry of Business, Innovation and Employment
MGP	Machine Graded Pine
MIG	Metal Inert Gas
MLS	Multiple Listing Sites
MMC	Modern Methods of Construction
MOU	Memorandum of Understanding
MPAC	Municipal Property Assessment Corporation
NALFA	North American Laminate Flooring Association
NatHERS	National House Rating Scheme
NBCC	National Building Code of Canada
NHER	National Home Energy Rating
NIOSH	National Institute for Occupational Safety and Health
NOFMA	National Oak Flooring Manufacturers Association
NRZ	Neutral Reach Zones
NZIA	New Zealand Institute of Architects
OHS	Occupational Health & Safety
ONS	Office for National Statistics
OSB	Oriented Strand Board
OSB (2)	Over Site Board

PHC	Passive House Canada
PHINZ	Passive House Institute New Zealand
PHIUS	Passive House Institute US
PHPP	Passive House Planning Package
PLF	Personnel + Logistical + Financial
PP Fibres	Polypropylene Fibres
PPVC	Prefabricated Prefinished Volumetric Construction
PUD	Planned Unit Development
QA + QC	Quality Assurance + Quality Control
RAIA	Royal Australian Institute of Architects
RAIC	Royal Architectural Institute of Canada
RESPA	Real Estate Settlement Procedures Act
RIAI	Royal Institute of Architects of Ireland
RIBA	Royal Institute of British Architects
RICS	Royal Institute of Chartered Surveyors
SAP	Standard Assessment Procedure
SAPS	Stand Alone Power System
SEAI	Sustainable Energy Authority of Ireland
SEAOC	Structural Engineers Association of California
SFL	Structural Floor Level
SHGC	Solar Heat Gain Coefficient
SHS	Square Hollow Section
SHT	Smart Home Technology
SMART	Simple, Measurable, Attainable, Relevant & Time Based
SS	Stainless Steel
SUDS	Sustainable Urban Drainage System
SWMS	Safe Working Method Statement
SWO	Stop Work Order
TBM	Temporary Bench Mark
TER	Target Emission Rate
TILA	Truth in Lending Act

TPO	Tree Preservation Order
UHI	Urban Heat Islands
USGBC	The U.S. Green Building Council
VE	Value Engineering
VR	Virtual Reality
VOC	Volatile Organic Compounds
WiFi	Wireless Fidelity
WSUD	Water Sensitive Urban Design
ZOI	Zone of Influence

SERVICES ABBREVIATIONS

AAV	Air Admitance Valve
AC	Alternating Current
AFDD	Arc Fault Detection Device
AFIC	Ark Fault Circuit Interrupters
ASHP	Air Source Heat Pump
CBE	Circuit Breaker Enclosure
CCTV	Close Circuit Television
CCU	Customer Consumer Unit
CCU (2)	Customer Control Unit
Cpc	Circuit Protective Conductor
DB	Distribution Board
DC	Direct Current
DP	Down Pipe aka Down Spout
EMF	Electromotive Force
GFCB	Ground Fault Circuit Breaker
GFCI	Ground Fault Circuit Interruptor
GSHP	Ground Source Heat Pump
IP	Ingress Protection
IR	Infra Red
LED	Light-emiting diode
MCB	Miniature Circuit Breaker
MH	Manhole
PES	Phantom Energy Stealer

PV	Photovoltaics
RCB	Residual Current Device
RWP	Rain Water Pipe
SAP	Stand Alone Power
SC	Stop Cock
SPD	Surge Protection Device
SS	Stub Stack
SVP	Soil & Ventilation Pipe
TMV	Thermostatic Mixing Valves

EXCAVATION GLOSSARY

Arcing	An electrical current that jumps a gap.
Backfill	Material to refill an open excavation.
Batter Board	Board used to fix a known mark or nail to indicate a set out line for a trench.
Battering	The formed, faced angled wall of an excavation.
Benching	Horizontal stepping to the side walls of an excavation.
Biodegradable Shuttering/Formwork	Shuttering that decomposes and effectively disappears leaving a void.
Hurdle	The name given to the batter board and staked legs used to fix a set out line.
Overburden	Surface soil to be removed.
Reactive Soil	Soil that shrinks when dry and swells when wet.
Sacrificial Formwork	Formwork left in place on completion - often buried.
Safe Slope	A formed face to the side of an excavation to prevent earth slippage.
Sheet Piling	Vertical interlocking or continuous excavation support.
Shoring	To support or prop.
Shuttering	A mould used to form concrete structures.
Slurry Mix	Colloquial term for weak and high water content concrete mix.
Step Foundation	Multi-levelled foundation that steps down in line with a site slope.

Trench Shield	Steel pre-formed braces moved into a trench for support.
Zone of Influence	An area affected by external loads e.g. Vehicles excavated materials etc.

PROFESSIONAL ROLES

Acoustic Engineer	A consultant who assesses sound emanating from a building or methods of sound blocking through design.
Air Test Engineer	A consultant who tests air tightness or air permeability of buildings.
Appraiser	A person who assesses (determines) the fair market value of a property. They can be employed by a realtor, mortgage company or other party.
Architects	Architects plan and design buildings. Their qualifications and registration vary in different jurisdictions but they are generally considered the most qualified designers of buildings.
Architectural Technicians	Usually employed by architects or act as consultants offering the services of a draughtspersons (draftspersons). They can have a very wide-ranging technical role.
Builder/General Contractor/ Main or Principal Contractor	A person or organisation that acts as a builder to others and enters into formal contracts to carry out the work.
Builders Quantity Surveyor/ Estimator	A surveyor who acts for the building contractor. An estimator is a surveyor who calculates costs for projects.

Building Biologist	Evaluates toxins, health hazards and provides strategies to avoid products with VOCs etc.
Building Inspectors/Building Control Officers/District Surveyors/ Building Official/Municipal or Town Inspector.	An inspector of the building process who confirms on completion that the works conform with local building codes. They may be private consultants or public employees depending upon jurisdiction.
Building Services Engineer	A consultant and designer of building services, water, electrical, air conditioning etc.
Building Surveyor	A surveyor who can inspect and report on a project or take control of the design and contract administration.
Bushfire Assessors (BAL Assessments) AU/NZ	A consultant employed to report on the Bushfire Attack Level (BAL) of a property or area. They are only required in certain jurisdictions.
Civil Engineer	Engineer who designs or supervises large public works such as bridges, tunnels, roads etc.
Clerk of Works	A person employed by the client to check on site practice and works quality.
Contract Manager	A person in charge of more than one construction site. He is often employed by a Principal Contractor.
Contractor /Trade Contractor/ Specialist Contractor	A person or organization taking control of a package of work or single trade on site but is not in control of the site.
Conveyancer	A professional who acts for you in the purchase of a property. Solicitors often undertake this work.

Cost Engineer	Similar to a PQS although found more in US & Canada. Involved in cost control/forecasting and investment appraisal.
Cost Manager	Can be referred to as Quantity Surveyor offers timely advice on costs to the client and Principal Designer throughout the project.
Craftspeople/Tradespeople	Someone who is skilled in a single trade.
Design and Manage/Design and Build	A single organisation is contracted to deliver the design as well as the construction works.
Domestic Client	People who have construction carried out on a property they own.
Domestic Subcontractor/Supplier	Contractors solely selected by the Principal Contractor.
Draughtsperson (Draftsperson)	They create technical drawings either by hand or computer aided designs (CAD). They plan and design buildings but are not usually as highly qualified as architects.
Electrical Engineers	Design electrical power installations including lighting, transformers and telecommunications.
Energy Assessors	A registered consultant who assesses the energy usage of a property or design. This is a government requirement in some jurisdictions.
Estate Agents	They act for the seller of a property and advertise and negotiate the sale on the sellers behalf. They do not work for the purchaser.

Fire Officers/Fire Consultants	Fire Officers usually work for the Fire Service or Local Government and assess fire risk and fire vehicle access issues. Fire consultants do the same on behalf of the constructor.
General Operatives/Labourers/ Laborers US	Unskilled or Semi Skilled worker.
Geotechnical Engineer/Soil Engineer	Engineers who assess the ground supporting capacity of a site. They supply this information to Structural Engineers.
Heritage Advisor	A consultant who advises and prepares reports as part of the planning process. It is used to provide additional information on the heritage impact of your design in the locality. This is only necessary in designated 'heritage areas'.
Interior Decorator	A designer who helps you dress a finished product with fabrics and furnishings, wall coverings etc.
Interior Designer	A designer who only works on the interior finish and 'look' of the internal spaces. They can advise at the brief stage over location of doors, windows etc. to assist with the efficient use of space and furnishings.
"Land Surveyor/Consulting Surveyor and Planner /Licensed Land Surveyor/ Land Development & Subdivision Consultants "	A surveyor who carries out topographical surveys and often defines specific land parcels and levels. Some offer subdivision and development advice.
Landscape Architects	External environments, gardens, parks, streetscapes etc.
Lawyer	See Solicitor.

Main Contractor	The person or organisation in charge of the actual work. Named from someone who signed or issues contracts for signing.
Management Contracting	A site manager who commits to manage a project not supply the construction works. By agreement they can provide work packages though trade /specialist contractors and receive funds to pass over for payment.
Monitoring Surveyor	A surveyor who acts for a lender and monitors site progress for fund release.
Multi-Skilled	Someone who is skilled in more than one trade. Often not formally qualified in each trade.
Named Sub Contractor/Supplier	Contractors approved by the client as acceptable. The Principal Contractor does not have to use them as he takes responsibility for their work.
Nominated Sub Contractor/Supplier	Contractors that the client instructs the Principal Contractor to employ.
Owner-Builder	See Self-Builder.
Partnering	Partnering is where two or more organisations commit to collaborative relationships as a one off or as an ongoing long-term arrangement.
Party Wall Surveyor	A surveyor who advises on party wall and adjoining building matters. He can either work for the constructor or neighbour.
Planner/City Planner/Urban Planner/Town Planner	A planner can work as a private consultant or for a local authority or government body. They advise on land use, building use, density, planning refusal and appeals etc.

Principal Contractor	The person or organisation that acts as the controller of the construction process on a building site. Appointed to be in control of more than one contractor.
Principal Designer /CDM Co-ordinator	A manager and co-ordinator for the Construction Design and Management aspects of the H&S obligations of the client, design team and contractors. This is a necessary role in some jurisdictions.
Professional Quantity Surveyor (PQS)	A surveyor who calculates quantities of materials, prepares specifications and organizes and advises on the tender process. They often act in a project management role and offer aligned services such as H&S advice.
Project Manager	A person who manages a large single project or a few separate projects.
Property Finder	A professional who locates property, often off-market sales, and assists the purchaser. Some Estate Agents offer this service.
Right of Light Surveyor	A surveyor who calculates the amount of light that a building will receive or shade after construction.
Self-Builder	A person who builds for themselves usually for owner occupation. See Owner-Builder.
Solicitor/Barrister/Lawyer	The catchall term is Lawyer. They advise and represent clients in a variety of legal matters.
Statutory Contractor/Infrastructure Supplier	Contractor qualified to work on statutory services in public and private places such as roads, sewers etc. Often a monopoly.

Structural Engineer	Engineers who design the structure of a building.
Sub-Contractor/Subs/Subbie	A contractor who agrees a contract with the General Contractor for a section of work.
Tree Officers, Species and Habitat Assessors, Botanists	Consultants who can work for local government or act as consultants to constructors.
Valuation Surveyor	Surveyors who recommend a fair market value for a property. They can work for vendors or purchasers but their main clients are either lenders who want an independent valuation for lending purposes or insurance companies for insurance / replacement values.
VDC Project Manager/BIM	Virtual Design-to-Construction Manager & Building Information Management Manager. A designer who models the whole concept-to-occupation process through digital representation.
Vendor/Seller	Seller of a property.
Worker/Operative	Someone who works under the instruction of a contractor/builder.

INDEX

3D Printing, 13
4IR, 13

A

Alexander, Christopher, 60
American Institute of Architects (AIA), xi
Architects, 101-2,213
Artificial Intelligence (AI), 13-14
Assemblage, 37
Auctions (Public), 49,75-76
Augmented Reality (AR), 13-14,

B

Brownfield Land, 27-28,48
Buildability, 128
Building Information Management (BIM), 13-14
Building Inspectors & Certifiers, 83

C

Closing, 75
Cold (Thermal) Bridging, 130
Compliant Permit, 72
Computer Aided Design (CAD), 14
Constructability, 128
Cost Engineer, 82,103
Cross Laminated Timber (CLT), 16

D

Designed for Manufacture and Assembly (DFMA), 16
Designers, 55,101-102,115,149

E

Easements, 43-45,68
Ecology and Biodiversity, 48
Elemental Cost Control, 166
Engineers, 11,108-110
Ergonomics, 127
External Lighting, 10-11

F

Finance, 47,67,163
Funding, 18,177-193

G

Gazumping, 45
Greenfield Land, 28
Gross Development Value (GDV), 39, 163-165

H

Habitat, 9,48
Home Energy Management System (HEMS), 19
Homeowners Association (HOA), 41-42

I

Integrated Project Delivery, xi
Interstate Purchase, 77
Infrastructure and Utility Companies, 84

K

Know Your Client (KYC), 74

L

Lien, 73
Lot and Block, 24-25
Lifetime Home Standards, 131

M

Metes and Bounds, 25
Modern Methods of Construction (MMC), 12
Modular Construction, 13-15

N

Neutral Reach Zones (NRZ), 126

O

Option, 45
Overage, 45

P

Package Builders, 110
Passive House, 130
Performance Gap, 12,132
'Perc' (Percolation) Test, 30
Permits, 35
Pre-Construction, 55
Professional Consultants, 82
Program, 55
Prosumers, 19
Public Footpaths, 42
Purchase Agreement, 74

R

Radon Gas, 48
Realtors, 35,44-46
Rectangular (Government) Survey, 25
Residual Valuation, 38-39
Restricted and Unrestricted Land, 30
Restrictive Conditions Covenants (RC&Cs), 41
Robotics, 13

S

Sherott, Ken, 60
Subdivision, 37,41
Superficial Method, 164-167
Sustainability, 129-130
Standard Assessment Process (SAP), 133
Specifications, 103-106,171

T

Tiny House, 12
Torrens Certificate, 25
Tree Ordinance, 46

U

Unit Method, 162

V

Value Engineering (VE), 134-139
Virtual Reality (VR), 13
Volumetric Construction, 15,17

W

Waste Plan, 7

Z

Zoning, 31-44,139

ABOUT THE AUTHOR

Born into a building family, Philip always had his eye on the trade. After leaving school, he joined a prestigious building company and went on to become a qualified building surveyor and a Member of the Chartered Institute of Building (MCIOB). Philip has acted as a consultant across the US as well as partnering with US based companies to develop projects in the Caribbean. He has completed projects in the UK, Ireland, Europe, North Africa and Australia. At the invitation of the US government, he has spoken to and met educational and trade association groups across the US regarding construction training and Modern Methods of Construction. Philip has worked on numerous 'special' new build residential projects and on many public & government buildings, railway infrastructure, retail, commercial, clinical & medical facilities and apartment blocks.

Over the years, Philip's company has won awards from the Royal Institute of British Architects, the Civic Trust, the Department of the Environment and the National House Builders Council (NHBC). He is an experienced public speaker and shares his take on current building matters and related topics. He has also supported and served as a board member of charities promoting training in the construction industry for young people and mid-career changers.

First and foremost, Philip is a builder.

Philip can be contacted directly at philip@abuilderscompanion.com

TAKE-AWAYS

"Knowledge without application is simply knowledge".
— Kasi Kaye Lilopoulos

These are listed in no particular order, as events can occur in any order, and any of the following tips may set you off on a train of thought. Please send me your tips to be included in a future revision.

- It's the ENVIRONMENT stupid; for all decisions select the renewable choice
- Focus on U-Values & R-Values – can they be easily and economically improved?
- If a gas service is to be installed – remember to design in an external ventilated boxing (as the unthought-of brightly coloured pipes on the external face look unsightly)
- Don't only look at a material for today – what will it look like in a few years?
- Will future purchasers of your home want it to be eco-friendly?
- Try to reduce, as far as possible, opening or penetrations in floors or roofs
- All steps on different stairs should be equal where possible
- Ask yourself 'how can I incorporate a pond?'
- Think of your 'travel distance' in kitchen design
- Go out of your way to look at different houses and their external finishes
- Can off-site production play a role?
- How much Smart House Technology do you choose to add?
- Consider how to design out harm to wildlife
- How low can you go when it comes to zero carbon footprint?
- What is your current GDV projection? - update regularly
- The cheapest energy is the energy you do not use!

- Do all areas have more than one purpose?
- Ask yourself 'what does over-design mean?'
- What history have you uncovered on the site?
- The three most important sets of documents are drawings, budget and schedule

DO YOU FEEL 'COMPANIONABLE'?

I hope you enjoyed The Builder's Companion Book 1, Zero to Building Permit. Can you please take a moment to share your review on the site you purchased this book and on social media (anywhere between two words and as many as you like) would be very helpful to me and benefit other owner–builder's to find the book.

Do you know of someone else with an interest in home building?

Have you thought of sending them a copy of the book or e-book?

I would be pleased if we can get the book out there.

Just drop me a line at philip@abuilderscompanion.com letting me know what you think and I will personally respond.

Everyone needs a building buddy or …The Builder's Companion.

Your companion for the second part of your build journey is available.

A building guide different to any other.

To assist your transition from planning permit to on-site building, your BONUS preview is exclusively available overleaf ....

INTRODUCTION

'If there was only one solution to every problem, the world would be insanely dull'.

– Kara Barbieri

Are you attempting the Everest of challenges: to build your own house on time and within budget? All the endless possibilities can seem overwhelming, but with the guidance here hopefully you'll feel empowered to make decisions. The purpose of this practical book is to help you as Owner-Builder whittle down your options and assist you to confidently give instructions.

The Builder's Companion comprises of two books. Book 1, Zero to Building Permit, introduces the stages and decision-making processes to be considered and acted on before building your new home. Planning and preparation must be rigorous to get the best result from your owner-build project.

This book focusses on all the things an owner-builder must know to build a modern, environmentally-sound home. It's best to be read while you're gathering information on home building and are becoming clearer on direction, but well before an on-site plumber asks you where a pipe should go!

Why are you building a new home or renovating an older home? There are many homes that are for sale in all conditions and styles and in all areas. Some owner-builders want the challenge and some want to be able to create their own home with their own hands... some just want a better house for less money. No idea is more worthy or important than any other; what is important is that you are committed to the project.

I have built homes and numerous other buildings around the world all my working life and sometimes feel that I have seen everything at least once! This is of course not true and we are always hearing of new ideas and building techniques. The world around us is changing fast and our homes become a mirror to this change as well as a response. Home-builders must design in the spaces and comforts that society has come to expect and we must, even when building a single home, respond to global challenges.

It is easy to believe that this is all for other people to concern themselves with. But if you want to meet ever tightening building regulations and codes, or will ever look to sell your property, then you must build in a manner that is aware of the expectations to only sustainably develop. In the-not-too distant future, a premium price will be paid for sustainable homes and a price drop for those needing retrofitting. It is always more expensive to upgrade a building than to construct it sustainably from the beginning.

The two books are part of 'A Builders Companion' series with the 'companion' part being the most important. The books are an aid for you to rely on and must be relevant to you as an owner-builder. There are innumerable technical points of information available on the internet, but the internet does not bring all the parts together to a single point. That is the role of the 'companion'.

First, let's review the processes of planning and purchase.

Plot purchase comes after discussions with consultants but before briefing consultants.

Securing a suitable plot for an as yet un-designed home is a real chicken-and-egg situation. You need answers to confirm your instinct to purchase, and yet you cannot get definitive answers to many questions over design and cost. Architects/designers/lawyers can at least advise on site suitability and try to tease out if it is suitable for your family needs.

When considering the purchase of a plot, you will be concerned as to its current zoning and planning status and will want to be confident your home designs will receive a building permit.

There are other practicalities too. Have you ensured all external boundaries are correct and rights do not extend to others over access and egress? Legal limitations are always followed by financial implications and so you must ensure you are at the right end of any deal.

Even before the brief, even before the purchase, you must be able to assure yourself that the whole project is financially feasible. At this stage, some questions to ask are: Have I allowed sufficient costs? and, what items should be included? What information do I still need to collect?

After purchase, matters are more serious and all major decisions affect all other decisions. Are you going to employ a builder or owner-build? How much emphasis must you place on project management? What tactics will you employ to meet the demands of building a fine home on time and within budget?

You will need a team of consultants, so who will you appoint? What can they do for you and how much will you need to budget for their fees? Do you need a consultant planner or can the designer take this role all the way through to the issue of a building permit?

It is important you consider all available options – along with the design direction you wish to go in – before you agree a program with your design team. For example, what do you think about ecological features, or say, the merits of timber cladding versus aluminum? How large a home would you prefer to build?

If you're up to the design program point, are you ready to discuss it? Which stages of the design will you achieve before agreement and freezing the scheme? Are all areas equal or do some have more functions than others? What are your planning professional's major responsibilities? Who are the other players affecting your design that you do not employ? Are these players committed to your project?

The program is a distillation of the vast range of options and opportunities available to you and points you in the direction of the intended size and style of the home.

The finished house will be a reflection of its owners; the choice of what it is and how it is built is one available for you to grasp with both hands. Building a home is not a passive option but in fact is one of the most exciting thing you can ever do!

> **TIP BOX**
>
> *Murphy's Law*
>
> Murphy's famous law is often termed as 'anything that can go wrong, will go wrong'. It is almost as if a mythical force takes over just to ruin whatever you are trying to achieve.
>
> There is another law, called the Samuel Goldwyn law, which states, 'The harder I work, the luckier I get'. This can be amended for the owner-builder to be 'the better I manage, the luckier I get'. As regards the owner-builder, things generally go wrong at certain stages. By effectively managing these stages, opportunities to mention Mr. Murphy decrease.

Murphy Avoidance Stages

Stage 1: Design.

- Have a clear overall design to be shared with those who need it.
- Listen to your consultants and contractors.
- Carefully look at overall designs and identify cross-over points between trades.
- Prepare larger scale details or written notes to cover these crossovers so people are clear on what to do.
- Within a trade, is there a certain way you would prefer something arranged? An example is: which specific lights you want connected to which specific switch. If so, make sure you communicate this on a drawing.
- Indicate routes you want services and drains, etc. to follow. This can be within the house or externally.
- Spray paint large numerals indicating datum levels spread across the site. This relates specified heights back to your build levels.

Stage 2: Site Organization.

- Keep a clean site.
- Materials are to be stored neatly and safely.
- Meet all Health and Safety (OH&S) requirements.
- Laminate copies of current drawings on site for reference.

- Tell everyone who will listen that you are pleased to discuss any points of the work they may not be crystal clear on.
- Repeat clear instructions to ensure the listener 'gets' your message.
- Update the schedule of works regularly.
- Keep in touch with contractors on site and those scheduled to attend.
- Keep in touch with suppliers and be across delivery issues.
- Be clear on what items of work need to be checked or certified as part of the building control process.
- Listen to what people are saying.
- Be a good neighbor.

Stage 3: Office.

- Keep a clean set of approved building permit drawings.
- Drawings and specifications are to be available as hard copies and electronic copies.
- Confirm all material orders in writing (electronically will be OK).
- Keep and file all delivery notes.
- Keep and file all receipts.
- Place all contractor orders in line with the decided contractual process.
- Personally, approve all invoices before payment.
- Prepare only high quality documents for your lender.
- Update costings regularly.
- Update cash flow regularly.
- Keep all warranties and product information in good order.

Things may still go wrong even if you follow up on each and every point listed… but Murphy's Law will have a much larger impact if you do not!

Introduction – Action

- Discuss your build in detail with your designers
- Learn the drawings and details
- Remember Occupational Health and Safety
- Draw up a Schedule of Works
- Cash-flow

Made in the USA
Las Vegas, NV
24 October 2023

79627912R00140